DISARMAMENT INSPECTION
UNDER SOVIET LAW

by

HAROLD J. BERMAN and PETER B. MAGGS

1967

OCEANA PUBLICATIONS, INC.

Dobbs Ferry, New York

ii

TABLE OF CONTENTS

iii

INTRODUCTION

This book is addressed to those who are interested in disarmament—including any measure to control the use, manufacture, stockpiling, or testing of arms; it is also addressed to those who are interested in the broader question of the kinds of changes that would be required in the major legal systems of the world in order to support the intense international cooperation that disarmament presupposes.

American proposals for extensive arm control or disarmament agreements have generally included provisions for inspection in the Soviet Union by an international organization or by the non-Soviet party or parties to the agreement, in order to verify compliance. Little attention has been given, however, to the fact that any on-site or aerial inspection would inevitably bring non-Soviet citizens—inspectors—into contact with Soviet law, and that this in turn would raise a number of serious questions concerning both the rights of the inspectors and the rights of Soviet citizens. An excellent book has been written by Louis Henkin dealing with the problems that would be created under American law by international inspection;[1] the present work, although it is much less detailed than Professor Henkin's, is offered partly as a companion-piece and as a step toward a comparative study of the practicality of international inspection from a legal point of view.

We know how difficult it is to keep peace even within our own country, with its common traditions and its common goals. We demand police protection—and complain bitterly about police abuse. How would we respond, then, if an international inspectorate made up of Soviet, African, German, Chinese, and other members, were to search American homes and factories, seize American property, and interrogate American citizens, for the purpose of determining whether weapons had been illegally manufactured or stored? Should there be no limits on their powers? On the other hand, how could their effectivenes and their safety be guaranteed? It is with these two questions that Professor Henkin's book was chiefly concerned.

Suppose the international inspectorate goes to the Soviet Union: the two questions remain, though one is tempted to put them in reverse order.

---

[1] Louis Henkin, *Arms Control and Inspection in American Law* (New York, 1958).

The questions compel us to examine the Soviet legal system. Suppose the international inspectors suspected that a certain Soviet official had certain information that would be valuable to the inspectorate: would Soviet law compel the official to answer questions? What are the penalties under Soviet law for refusal to answer? Could the inspectors go to the official's house and tear it apart to find secret documents? Could they give him a lie detector test, or question him at night under a bright light? (It is of some interest that the 1960 Russian Code of Criminal Procedure expressly forbids interrogation of criminal suspects and accused persons at night, no doubt partly in a reaction against the methods of the state security agencies under Stalin.) Could the inspectors dig up a graveyard to find out if atomic weapons are hidden under it? (The 1960 Russian Criminal Code makes desecration of a grave punishable by deprivation of freedom up to three years.) Could the inspectors be prosecuted for crimes or sued for damages? Would even diplomatic immunity protect them against such hazards? Could they import inspection equipment, including bulldozers, boats, and the like, in their own aircraft, without special permission in each case? Suppose they accidentally came across classified information having no bearing on arms control or disarmament: could they divulge such information without violating Soviet criminal law? If not, what measures of enforcement are available to the Soviet authorities?

It may be thought that legal questions such as these are only academic, since the Soviet government could easily change its law, if necessary, to conform to the terms of any disarmament agreement that it wished to support. The problem, however, is not so simple. Many of the impediments to inspection posed by existing Soviet law are rooted in the nature of the Soviet legal and political system and could not be eliminated without considerable effort and imagination, and possibly not at all.

Moreover, one must know in advance what laws need to be changed and what changes would be adequate, under any of a broad range of inspection procedures, in order to formulate realistic inspection proposals. We cannot negotiate for disarmament on the simple assumption that inspectors should be free to roam the Soviet Union at will and do what they like, without restriction or liability. At the same time, we must seek to anticipate the possible use of Soviet domestic legal doctrines and restraints either to prevent or to frustrate inspections undertaken pursuant to disarmament agreement.

In addition, knowledge of Soviet law can be important in negotiations of disarmament arrangements, since discussion of Soviet legal impediments to such arrangements can help to test Soviet intentions and to bring home to Soviet negotiators the extent to which effective inspection procedures would require changes in the Soviet system of law and government. Indeed, there is no better way of bringing reality into disarmament negotiations than to seek solutions to the specific problems that enforcement would pose for the domestic legal and political systems of the contracting parties, while recognizing that an agreement might be desirable even if not all those problems are solvable.

Yet even if they were all solvable, there remains the question whether it is worth while to discuss them. A disarmament agreement would seem to be only a remote possibility in a world so badly divided as ours. Is not talk of disarmament, therefore, a utopian distraction from the real tasks that confront us? Indeed, it may be. Yet it may also be one of those distractions that enable us to halt, at least, on the edge of the abyss and consider alternative paths, even if we cannot see very clearly or very far along them. The analysis of disarmament problems, in other words, may have a value independent of the possibility, or even the desirability, of achieving disarmament. Such analysis may help us to understand the kinds of adjustment that all nations must make in their institutions and, more important, in their thinking, if we are ever to have peace in the world.

We would stress, then, that the underlying concern of this book is not with disarmament as such, or with inspection as such—although the legal problems of inspection form the main subject of our investigation—but with law, and particularly with law as a channel for, and an obstacle to, cooperation between nations that would like to cooperate with each other but do not know how. Even if a disarmament agreement is never reached, a study of the problems of inspection under Soviet law has both practical and theoretical value, because it brings into a focus the entire Soviet system of rules and procedures applicable to a foreign presence in Soviet territory. The legal problems that would confront international inspectors in the Soviet Union are closely related to the legal problems that now confront foreigners who go there for the purpose of engaging in diplomacy, trade, education, research, cultural relations, tourism, or other activities. We have therefore conceived of this book as a case study in peace, believing that its subject matter has much to teach concerning the role of law in overcoming international conflict—not, to be sure, at the level of high foreign policy, but at the level of basic rules of conduct directly affecting persons engaged in international relations in a public or private capacity.

I.

GENERAL CHARACTERISTICS OF SOVIET LAW RELEVANT TO INSPECTION

The limited scope of this study precludes any detailed discussion of the Soviet legal system as a whole.[2] However, certain general aspects of Soviet law that have particular relevance to inspection should be mentioned. These are (a) the unitary nature of the Soviet political and legal systems; (b) Soviet law as a means of forming Soviet public opinion and attitudes; (c) the incorporation of treaty norms in Soviet domestic legislation; and (d) the problem of secret legislation.

A. THE UNITARY NATURE OF THE SOVIET POLITICAL AND LEGAL SYSTEMS

A cursory reading of the texts of the Constitutions of the United States and of the Soviet Union[3] would show many similarities. Both Constitutions establish federal systems; both provide for legislative, executive and judicial branches; both provide civil rights and civil liberties. Closer examination, however, would show that the two Constitutions are the embodiment of radically different political theories. The American theory of checks and balances stands in contrast to the Soviet theory of a monolithic or hierarchical state, in which both the legal system and the political system are unified and the two systems are unified with each other.

The unity of the legal system is embodied in a number of principles of Soviet constitutional and statutory law. Although the Constitution establishes a division of functions between the federal ("all-union") authority and that of the fifteen union republics, the grant of powers to the federal

---

2. General works on the Soviet legal system are listed in the Bibliography, *infra* p. 146.
3. *Konstitutsiia (Osnovnoi zakon) Soiuza Sovetskikh Sotsialisticheskikh Respublik* (Moscow, 1964), as amended, Dec. 11, 1964, *Vedomosti*, 1964, no. 51, item 575, and October 2, 1965, Vedomosti, 1965, no. 39, item 559; English translation: *Constitution (Fundamental Law) of the Union of Soviet Socialist Republics* (Moscow, 1962). Soviet treatises on constitutional law include A. Denisov and M. Kirichenko, *Soviet State Law* (Moscow, 1960) and A. I. Lepeshkin, *Kurs sovetskogo gosudartvennogo prava {Textbook of Soviet State Law}*, Vol. 1 (Moscow, 1961); Vol. II (Moscow, 1962). Relevant articles from the Constitution are printed in the Documentation, *infra* pp. 51-58.

authority is so broad as to bring all major governmental problems within its competence; moreover, the virtual omnicompetence of the federal authority is matched by a virtually unlimited responsibility to regulate all major aspects of Soviet political, economic, and social life. Thus Article 14 of the Constitution defines federal jurisdiction as including not only such traditional functions of central government as the conduct of foreign affairs, the organization of national defense, the safeguarding of state security, the direction of the monetary and credit systems, and the like, but also the conduct of foreign trade on the basis of state monopoly, the determination of the national economic plans of the USSR, and the administration of industrial, agricultural, and trading enterprises and institutions of all-union importance. Taken together with Article 6, which provides that land and the means of production shall be state property, this signifies that the federal authority not only regulates but also operates a large part of the Soviet economy. Article 14 also assigns to the federal authority the jurisdiction to legislate in the spheres of education and public health, labor, the judicial system, criminal and civil law and procedure, and marriage and the family. Here, too, jurisdiction presupposes not only a power to legislate but also a responsibility to legislate. Moreover, since there is no doctrine of judicial review of the constitutionality of federal legislation, the scope of Soviet legislation is limited politically only by the self-restraint of the legislator.

It is also important to note that although the supreme legislative authority, under the Constitution, is vested in the Supreme Soviet of the USSR (Articles 30 and 32), virtually all the powers of the Supreme Soviet are also exercised by its Presidium, which meets between sessions of the parent body. Under Article 49 of the Constitution, the Presidium has the power to issue edicts (*ukazy*), and these have the force of law, although they are subject to ratification by the Supreme Soviet. In fact, the Supreme Soviet is a very large body (some 2000 members), which generally meets only twice a year for less than a week at a time, while the Presidium is a small body (33 members), which generally meets regularly throughout the rest of the year. There has never been an instance when the Supreme Soviet did not unanimously ratify the edicts of its Presidium.

The executive authority of the Soviet state is exercised by the Council of Ministers of the USSR, a body consisting of a Chairman, the First Deputy Chairmen, the Deputy Chairmen, the chairmen of the Republican Councils of Ministers *ex-officio*, and the heads of about sixty ministries and government agencies. The Council of Ministers issues "decrees" (*post-*

4

anovleniia) implementing the "laws" (*zakony*) of the Supreme Soviet and the "edicts" (*ukazy*) of the Presidium of the Supreme Soviet. Under Article 68 of the Constitution, such decrees cover an enormous range of activities and they are, in fact, the operative legislation whereby the Soviet economy and much of the day-to-day life of Soviet society are regulated. Theoretically, a decree of the Council of Minsiters that violated a law or a provision of the Constitution would be invalid and subject to annulment by the Presidium of the Supreme Soviet [Article 49(f)], but no decree seems ever to have been challenged on such grounds, although at least one (the introduction of fees for secondary and higher education in 1940) was clearly contrary to the Constitution, which at that time stated that education shall be free. (Later the Constitution was amended to conform to the decree!).[4]

The members of the Supreme Court of the USSR are chosen by the Supreme Soviet for a term of five years. The Supreme Court exercises control—through the decision of cases and the issuing of instructions to lower courts—over the application of the law; it may declare legislative or executive acts of republican supreme soviets or republican councils of Ministers to be unconstitutional, but, as already indicated, it has no right to do so in the case of legislative acts of the USSR Supreme Soviet and no de facto power to do so in the case of executive acts of the USSR Council of Ministers. Indeed, decisions of the USSR Supreme Court may be annulled by the Presidium of the USSR Supreme Soviet [Article 49(c)].

Finally, the unity of the legal system is supported by the Procuracy of the USSR, a very large but highly centralized organization whose principal task—in addition to the prosecution of criminal cases in court—is to protest to higher administrative agencies illegal acts of subordinate agencies.[5] The Procurator General of the USSR is chosen for a term of

4. Cf. M. Mikhailov, "Nekotorye voprosy sovetskoi konstitutsionnoi praktiki" [Some Problems of Soviet Constitutional Practice], *Sovetskoe gosudarstvo i pravo [Soviet State and Law}*, 1956, no. 9, p. 3, at p. 10, note 3.
5. The powers and duties of the procuracy are governed by the Polozhenie o prokurorskom nadzore v SSSR [Statute on Procuratorial Supervision in the USSR], *Vedomosti*, 1955, no. 9, item 222; as amended, *id.*, 195, no. 9 item 67; *id.*, 1960, no. 10, item 65; *id.*, 1964, no. 8, item 100. English translation: CDSP, Vol. VII, no. 23 (July 20, 1955), pp. 3-5. A good Soviet book on the procuracy is S. G. Berezovskaia, *Okhrana prav grazhdan Sovetskoi prokuraturoi [Protection of the Rights of Citizens by the Soviet Procuracy}* (Moscow, 1964). Non-Soviet commentary includes D. A. Loeber, "The Soviet Procuracy and the Rights of the Individual Against the State," *Journal of the International Commission of Jurists*, Vol. I, (1957), pp. 59-105; Glenn Morgan, *Soviet Administrative Legality: the Role of the Attorney General's Office* (Stanford, 1962); Harold J. Berman, *Justice in the USSR: An Interpretation of Soviet Law* (Cambridge, Mass., 1963), pp. 238-247; Harold J. Berman and James W. Spindler, *Soviet Criminal Law and Procedure: The RSFSR Codes* (Cambridge, Mass., 1966), pp. 109-117.

seven years by the Supreme Soviet; he appoints his subordinates, who in turn name their subordinates subject to his confirmation. The Procuracy of the USSR exercises what is called "general supervision" of the constitutionality and legality of administrative acts by all agencies up to but not including the highest republican and all-union authorities; it also supervises the legality of judicial decisions by protesting such decisions to higher courts, up to the Plenum of the Supreme Court of the USSR.

It is apparent from the above outline that the formal structure of the Soviet legislative, executive, and judicial branches itself contains built-in protections against conflicts among the top agencies of authority. This unity is further strengthened by the ease with which any recalcitrant members of the three branches can be removed. For example, if a member of the Supreme Soviet should ever vote against legislation proposed by the Communist Party leadership (none has ever done so thus far), he could without difficulty be removed by a recall election conducted in accordance with Article 142 of the Constitution and with the Law on the Procedure for the Recall of a Deputy of the Supreme Soviet.[6] Under the Statute on the Supreme Court of the USSR, members of that court may be removed by decision of the Presidium of the Supreme Soviet, and other laws provide similar means for removal of lower court judges.[7] Members of the USSR Council of Ministers may be released at any time by the Presiduim of the Supreme Soviet (Article 49(g) of the Constitution), and all lower executive officials may be dismissed by the head of the ministry or government department for which they work.[8]

The unity of the political system is embodied in the monopoly of the Communist Party over all political activities, and in the strict subordination of lower organizations to higher organizations in the Party hierarchy. The

---

6. O poriadke otzyva deputata Verkhovnogo Soveta [On the Procedure for the Recall of a Deputy of the Supreme Soviet] *Vedomosti,* 1959, no. 44, item 222, discussed in Lepeshkin, *supra* note 3, pp. 362-367.
7. Article 18 of the Polozhenie o Verkhovnom Sude SSSR [Statute on the Supreme Court of the USSR], *Vedomosti,* 1957, no. 4, item 85 (English translation: Denisov and Kirichenko, *supra* note 3, p. 438 at p. 443), states: "The President, Deputy President, and members of the Supreme Court of the USSR, as well as the people's assessors of the Supreme Court of the USSR, may be released from their duties prior to the expiration of their term of office only by a decision of the Supreme Soviet of the USSR, and in the intervals between its sessions by a decision of the Presidium of the Supreme Soviet of the USSR subject to subsequent confirmation by the Supreme Soviet of the USSR." No grounds for removal or other substantive limitations upon the power of removal are given.
8. Procedures for the summary dismissal of officials are given in Polozhenie o poriadke rassmotreniia trudovykh sporov [Statute on the Procedure for Examining Labor Disputes], *Vedomosti,* 1957, no. 4, item 58, Appendix I, as amended, *Vedomosti,* 1960, no. 2, item 6; English translation: U.S. Department of Labor, Bureau of Labor Statistics, *Principal Current Soviet Labor Legislation* (Washington, 1962), pp. 99-100.

Soviet Communist Party is not a political party at all in the American sense of that term. Political parties, in the sense of groups openly competing with each other for public office, do not exist in the USSR. The Communist Party is, rather, a huge elite corps, consisting, according to Article 126 of the Constitution, of "the most active and politically conscious citizens." The Central Committee of the Communist Party, consisting of some 200 persons, and the Politburo of the Central Committee, consisting now of 11 persons, make the basic decisions concerning all aspects of Soviet life; the intermediate leaders and the rank and file, consisting of about 12 million persons, are a highly disciplined organization whose task is to implement those decisions.

The unity between the political and legal systems is ensured by the principle of Party control of all governmental agencies, a principle expressed in Article 126, which provides that the Communist Party is "the leading core of all organizations, both social and state." In one sense, therefore, the Party is outside the governmental structure, independent of it, with its own organization, its own leadership, its own *raison d'être,* while in another sense the Party is inside the governmental structure, guiding and directing it in all its work. At the summit of the two hierarchies of Party and State, they merge: the present Chairman of the Council of Ministers, A. N. Kosygin, and the present President of the Presidium of the Supreme Soviet, N. V. Podgornyi, are top leaders in the Politburo of the Central Committee of the Communist Party, under its present General Secretary L. I. Brezhnev. At lower levels the Party and State hierarchies are usually kept separate in an organizational sense, although important governmental officials at all levels are almost invariably Party members.

Party control over the Soviet governmental structure has led many people to doubt that law can play an important part either in Soviet domestic life or in Soviet international relations. Surely, in a society where law is officially viewed as an instrument of Communist Party policy there cannot be the same degree of legal security and legal stability as in societies where law is viewed as having a life of its own, which is independent of and superior to the political leadership. Yet as Soviet history has demonstrated, the Soviet Communist Party has again and again been compelled by its own interests to bow to law, even though in a deeper sense it is not bound by it. In fact, the Soviet leaders have learned from long and hard experience, both domestic and international, that it is impossible to achieve their aims without a highly developed stable legal system. Even Stalin called for "stability of laws," and his successors have made legality one of the cornerstones of their policy. We shall be considering in detail, in later chapters, various provisions of Soviet criminal law, civil law, court procedure, administrative law and procedure, international law, and the like—most of which have very great importance in Soviet society; they are by no means window-dressing and they do in fact, if only by virtue of their technical legal complexity, have a certain life of their own which is independent of, though not always superior to, the political leadership. In stressing, at the outset of our study, the interdependence of law and policy in the Soviet system, we do not wish to prejudice the reader against our principal thesis—namely, that Soviet law can be an important means for the practical realization of a system of inspection under a disarmament agreement. We do wish, however, to make clear that Soviet law, by its own terms, is to a very high degree responsive to the will of the highest political leaders.

The unitary nature of the Soviet political and legal system has several important implications for an inspection arrangement under an arms control or disarmament agreement. First, if the Soviet leaders seriously wished to implement such an arrangement, they would encounter few formal legal obstacles. Even if amendments to the Constitution were required, this would not create legal difficulties of the magnitude that similar changes would involve in the United States. The Soviet Constitution, under Article 146, can be amended by a two-thirds majority of the Supreme Soviet — which, for reasons already indicated, would not be hard to obtain. Indeed, the Supreme Soviet has not shown any reluctance to amend the Constitution in the past; such amendments have been extremely frequent.[9] In fact there have been three different Constitutions in Soviet history (1918, 1924, and 1936),[10] and in 1962 a commission was appointed to present a new Constitution.[11] But even if it were not desired to amend the Constitution formally, it would be possible to secure a de facto amendment through an edict of the Presidium of the Supreme Soviet—a Soviet constitutional practice which has often been used in the past.[12]

Second, in view of the monolithic quality of Soviet politics and law, no legal devices could be expected to ensure the continued operation of the

---

9. See Lepeshkin, *supra* note 3, Vol. I. pp. 172-175.
10. See S. S. Studenikin, general editor, *Istoriia sovetskoi Konstitutsii (v dokumentakh), 1917-1956 gg. [A History of the Soviet Constitution (in documents), 1917-1956]* (Moscow, 1957).
11. O vyrabotke proekta novoi Konstitutsii SSSR [On the Preparation of a Draft of a New Constitution of the USSR], *Vedomosti*, 1962, no. 17, item 182; CDP, Vol. XIV, no. 17 (May 23, 1962), p. 8. N. S. Khrushchev was replaced by L. I. Brezhnev as chairman of the commission charged with drawing up the new constitution, by decrees of December 11, 1964. *Vedomosti*, 1964, no. 51, items 572 and 573.
12. See M. Mikhailov, *supra* note 4, p. 10.

inspection system once the leaders of the Soviet state decided it should be terminated. Technically, it would be as easy to repeal provisions of the Soviet Constitution and Soviet laws as it would be to pass them in the first place.

Third, the proper enforcement of legal arrangements would depend to a high degree on the willingness of the Soviet leadership to permit such enforcement at the time it were sought. This is not to say that proper legal arrangements could not be of great influence in securing continuing acceptance of an inspection system; on the contrary, as will be seen in subsequent portions of this book, appropriate legal arrangements could help not only to make the system acceptable to the Soviet leadership to begin with, but also to create political pressures for its proper enforcement and against its termination.[13] But in view of the subordination of all Soviet law enforcement agencies to the Communist Party leadership, it would be foolish to suppose that any legal arrangements could withstand the determination of that leadership not to abide by them.

B. SOVIET LAW AS A MEANS OF FORMING PUBLIC OPINION AND ATTITUDES

An important aspect of the Soviet legal system is the conscious use of law to secure moral and intellectual support on the part of the Soviet people, including Soviet officialdom, for the policies of the leadership.[14]

The Soviet Constitution is a primary vehicle for such indoctrination, which takes many forms, including a compulsory course on the Constitution taught in all Soviet secondary schools.[15] Therefore it might be a matter of considerable significance if the Constitution were amended to include express provisions committing the Soviet state to adherence to disarmament treaties and stating the authority of the inspection organization. The Soviet public would thus be taught the importance of aiding the inspection system in its operations and the illegality of attempting to cheat. If the Soviet leadership should issue secret orders to hinder the work of the inspection organization, without first securing a formal repeal of the Constitutional provisions guaranteeing its operations, the prior instruction of a large body of Soviet

13. See Roger Fisher, "Internal Enforcement of International Rules," in Seymour Melman, editor, *Disarmament: Its Politics and Economics* (Boston, 1962), p. 9, where a convincing argument is made for the enforcement of international rules by means proven effective for bringing domestic law to bear on governments.
14. Cf. Berman, *supra* note 5, Part 3.
15. Content and teaching methods of this course are discussed in G. P. Davydov and V. I. Mazurenko, *Prepodavanie Konstitutsii SSSR v shkole {Teaching the Constitution of the USSR in School}* (D. S. Karev, ed., 2nd enl. ed., Moscow, 1961).

citizens in the illegality of such orders might cause it some difficulty. In addition, the existence of a widespread body of opinion, officially induced, in favor of the continued support of the legal rights of the inspection system would be a factor which the leadership would have to weigh if it ever considered the formal abrogation of the inspection arrangements and the repeal of the relevant sections of the Constitution. The repeal of these sections of the Constitution, if it did come about, would serve as a clear signal of Soviet intention to withdraw from the disarmament arrangement, and so could form an acceptable justification for whatever retaliatory or compensatory measures the other parties to the arrangement might wish to take.

Similar considerations would apply to the inclusion of references to the inspection organization in the Rules of the Communist Party of the Soviet Union, which are, in effect, a second Soviet constitution. Indeed, in view of the "leading role" of the party, the inclusion of such references in its Rules woud have as great value as their inclusion in the Constitution.

It would also be important, in terms of the educational role of Soviet law, to secure the inclusion of clear and direct references to the powers of the inspection organization in many Soviet statutes and regulations that govern activities related to those that the inspection organization would perform. Such inclusion would be in accordance with normal Soviet practice, as indicated below.

C. THE INCORPORATION OF TREATY NORMS IN SOVIET DOMESTIC LEGISLATION

Many provisions of Soviet domestic law provide for the application of treaty norms. Some directly incorporate the language or spirit of the treaty; others provide in general terms for the application of past, present, and future treaty norms.

The first method is used particularly in criminal law, where a general reference to the treaty would be too vague to provide adequate notice to potential violators. A number of examples of the inclusion of specific treaty provisions in Soviet domestic law may be found in the Law on Criminal Responsibility for Military Crimes.[16] Thus, in compliance with

16. Zakon ob ugolovnoi otvetstvennosti za voinskie prestupleniia, *Vedomosti*, 1959, no. 1, item 10, *CDSP*, Vol. XI, no. 5 (March 11, 1959), pp. 4-7. See A. G. Gornyi, editor, *Nauchno-prakticheskii kommentarii k zakonu ob ugolovnoi otvetstvennosti za voinskie prestupleniia {Scholarly and Practical Commentary to the Law on Criminal Liability for Military Crimes}* (2nd ed., Moscow, 1961); Bernard A. Ramundo, "Soviet Criminal Legislation in Implementation of the Hague and Geneva Conven-

international conventions relating to the Red Cross, Article 31 of this law makes it a crime punishable by deprivation of freedom from three months to a year to wear, without a right to do so, insignia of the Red Cross or Red Crescent in an area of military operations or to abuse in wartime the flags or insignia of the Red Cross or Red Crescent or the color identifying transport vehicles for medical evacuation.

The same method is also used for incorporating into Soviet civil procedure the complex provisions of treaties providing for legal assistance in civil cases. A lengthy decree of the Supreme Court of the USSR, binding upon all Soviet courts, gives precise instructions for the application of the provisions of those treaties.[17] This decree exemplifies the ability of the Soviet state to adapt its legal system to the detailed needs of Soviet international relations. The decree begins with a list of the treaties in force and a list of Soviet judicial and other agencies affected. There then follow ten pages of detailed instructions to these agencies on the application of the various treaties in various situations. An appendix of six pages of forms is designed to ensure convenience and uniformity in the administration of the decree.

A typical example of a general provision requiring the application of treaty norms may be found in Article 129 of the USSR Fundamental Principles of Civil Legislation,[18] which states that if an international treaty or an international agreement to which the USSR is a party establishes rules other than those which are contained in Soviet civil legislation, then the rules of the international treaty or international agreement shall be applied. Other examples are discussed in connection with later portions of this book.

tions Relating to the Rules of Land Warfare," *American Journal of International Law,* Vol. 57 (1963), p. 63. This law is incorporated almost verbatim in Articles 237-269 of the Criminal Code of the RSFSR, relevant portions of which are printed in the Documentation, *infra* pp. 102-104.

17. Decree of June 19, 1959, no. 2, *Sbornik postanovlenii Plenuma Verkhovnogo Suda SSSR,* 1924-1963 (*A Collection of Decrees of the Plenum of the Supreme Court of the USSR,* 1924-1963] (Moscow, 1964) p. 114.

18. Osnovy grazhdanskogo zakonodatel'stva Soiuza SSSR i Soiuznykh Respublik [Fundamental Principles of Civil Legislation of the USSR and the Union Republics], *Vedomosti,* 1961, no. 50, item 525, *id.,* 1962, no. 15, item 156. English translations: *CDSP* Vol. XIV, no. 4 (February 21, 1962), pp. 3-13; *Soviet Civil Legislation and Procedure, Official Texts and Commentaries* (Moscow, [1964?]), pp. 55-112; University of Leyden, *Law in Eastern Europe,* no. 7 (Leyden, 1963), pp. 263-298. The standard Soviet commentary is S. N. Bratus' and E. A. Fleishits, editors, *Nauchno-prakticheskii kommentarii k osnovam grazhdanskogo zakonodatel'stva Soiuznykh Respublik {A Scholarly and Practical Commentary to the Fundamental Principles of Civil Legislation of the USSR and the Union Republics}* (Moscow, 1962). The civil code of each of the fifteen Soviet republics incorporates and amplifies the provisions of the Fundamental Principles. An English translation of the RSFSR Civil Code, as well as the official Russian text, is contained in Whitmore Gray, ed., *Soviet Civil Legislation* (Ann Arbor, 1965).

In the light of these examples, it would seem worth while to consider how the rights of international or adversary inspectors, as spelled out in any proposed disarmament treaty or agreement, could be incorporated in Soviet domestic legislation. Of special importance in this connection would be the amendment of Soviet laws and administrative regulations so as to provide expressly for cooperation with such inspectors and for enforcement of their rights. Each of the Soviet state agencies upon which inspectors would depend for obtaining access to the Soviet Union and for carrying out their functions on Soviet territory is governed by a statute *(polozhenie)* stating its duties and powers. In addition, there are similar statutes governing the duties and powers of law-enforcement agencies, especially the police,[19] the courts,[20] and the procuracy.[21] Ways in which such statutes could be amended to protect the inspectors—either by direct incorporation of, or by general reference to, a disarmament treaty—will become apparent in the later discussion of the concrete problems which the inspectors would face.

D. SECRET LEGISLATION

The incorporation of the rights of inspectors in published Soviet laws can be effective only to the extent that the published laws are not superseded by later secret legislation. The existence of a tradition of secret legislation is one of the most serious legal problems that would face an inspection organization operating in the Soviet Union.

Since Stalin's death in 1953 there has been a very considerable improvement in the practice of publishing laws. Nevertheless, it remains true that many legal norms affecting the actions of Soviet officials, and even of Soviet courts, are not published, but are merely transmitted directly to those who must carry them out.[22] According to Soviet administrative law, officials are expected to obey instructions from their superiors, even if such instructions are in apparent conflict with published laws and regulations, until

---

19. See, *e.g.,* Polozhenie o Ministerstve Vnutrennikh Del RSFSR [Statute on the Ministry of Internal Affairs of the RSFSR], enacted by decree of the Council of Ministers of the RSFSR of April 25, 1961, no. 458, SP RSFSR, 1961, no. 12, item 47, as printed in *Sbornik normativnykh aktov po sovetskomu administrativnomu pravu {Collection of Normative Acts on Soviet Administrative Law}* (A. G. Khazikov, compiler, Moscow, 1964), p. 504. In 1962 the Ministry was renamed the "Ministry for the Protection of Public Order of the RSFSR." *RSFSR Vedomosti,* 1962, no. 35, item 535.
20. Statute on the Supreme Court of the USSR, *supra* note 6. Each of the union republics has passed a statute governing its judicial system. These are printed with a commentary in *Zakonodatel'stvo o sudoustroistive Soiuza SSR i soiuzynkh respublik {Legislation on the Judicial System of the USSR and the Union Republics}* (F. I. Kalinychev, ed., Moscow, 1961). The Law on Court Organization of the RSFSR is translated in Berman and Spindler, *supra* note 5.
21. *Supra* note 5.
22. Berman, *supra* note 5, at pp. 205-208, 235-236; on secret laws in the period prior to Stalin's death, see Vladimir Gsovski, *Soviet Civil Law,* Vol. I (Ann Arbor, 1948), pp. 224-229.

such time as the instructions are countermanded or rescinded by appropriate authorities, unless the instructions are criminal or grossly *ultra vires.*[23]

In accordance with a 1958 edict[24] and a 1959 decree,[25] those laws and decrees which are "of a normative character" or are "of general significance" are subject to regular publication. In practice this standard gives the authority passing a law or issuing an administrative decree considerable power to determine whether or not a given legal act should be published, since the concept of what is "normative" or "general" is quite flexible. A further problem is created by the fact that even the published decrees of the Council of Ministers of the USSR as well as those of the councils of ministers of the union republics, are not regularly available outside the USSR, and the decrees of individual ministries are not easily obtained even within the USSR. Very broad legislative power is granted to the Council of Ministers of the USSR by Article 68 of the Constitution of the USSR and to the republican councils of ministers by the republican constitutions; indeed, the decrees of the USSR and republican councils of ministers are called "legislation" *(zakonodatel'stvo)* in Soviet legal literature, although they are, technically, not "laws" *(zakony).* Also individual ministries are often granted *de facto* legislative powers by their charters. As a result there is a tremendous and growing body of executive legislation that would not be easy for the inspectorate to obtain.

The existence of unpublished legislation, and the requirement that it be obeyed when it conflicts with the published law, could create serious problems for an inspectorate. No matter how clearly its rights were expressed in published Soviet legislation, there would remain the possibility that the Soviet officials with whom it would have to deal might be under secret orders to sabotage its activities. It is for this reason that the following sections will place considerable emphasis upon those situations in which inspection organizations would need the active cooperation of Soviet officials.

A second and perhaps more serious consequence of the practice of withholding publications of laws and regulations that are not "normative" or "of general significance" is that it can cause difficulty in establishing the existence of a clear-cut violation of an inspection agreement, for the inspectors might have no way of knowing or proving that the difficulties they encounter are the result of the official policy of the Soviet government and not merely due to the mistakes or the inefficiency of local authorities.

---

23. *Sovetskoe administrativnoe pravo (obshchaia chast') {Soviet Administrative Law (General Part)}* (Iu. M. Kozlov, editor, Moscow, 1962), pp. 220-223.
24. Printed in the Documentation, *infra* p. 108.
25. Printed in the Documentation, *infra* p. 110.

II.

PRIVILEGES AND IMMUNITIES
OF THE INSPECTORATE

The definition of the privileges and immunities to be accorded to the inspection organization and to its personnel involves serious and complex problems of Soviet law. As will be pointed out in the following discussion, the mere grant of diplomatic privileges and immunities, while perhaps necessary, would by no means be sufficient.

The first section that follows will consider the privileges and immunities now granted by Soviet law: (1) to international organizations; (2) to foreign states and their agencies; (3) to foreign diplomats; and (4) to aliens and stateless persons. Next, the specific privileges and immunities that would be needed by an inspection organization and its personnel will be discussed in the light of present Soviet law, in order to identify what kinds of changes in the law would be required in order to safeguard the inspectorate.

A. PRIVILEGES AND IMMUNITIES NOW GRANTED BY SOVIET LAW

(1) *International Organizations.* The Soviet Union has by treaty granted certain privileges and immunities to a number of international and regional organizations. Notable examples are the Convention on the Privileges and Immunities of the United Nations,[26] and the Convention on the Legal Capacity, Privileges and Immunities of the Council for Mutual Economic Assistance.[27] Many of the provisions of these two conventions are identical or similar; in the absence of a study of the details of actual Soviet practice under them, however, it is not possible to determine whether or not there are substantial differences in the Soviet treatment of Communist and non-Communist international organizations even when the general rule is the same for both types.

---

26. Printed in the Documentation, *infra* p. 140.
27. Printed in the Documentation, *infra* p. 137.

It would be worth while to consider the possibility of using the Convention on the Privileges and Immunities of the United Nations as the legal basis for the functioning of an international inspectorate. United Nations disarmament inspectors admitted into the Soviet Union would be entitled, under the Convention, to "be accorded such privileges and immunities as are necessary for the independent exercise of their functions during the period of their missions, including the time spent on journeys in connection with their missions." (Article 22). Under the Convention, United Nations property would be immune from search and seizure, and United Nations representatives would enjoy personal immunity while exercising their functions. Lesser degrees of immunity would apply to officials of the United Nations and experts on missions for the United Nations. If the Convention could be used to implement an inspection arrangement by appropriate United Nations action, it would not be necessary for the Soviet Union to undertake any new treaty commitments. Thus the Soviets might be spared the embarrassment of entering treaty arrangements that might be unacceptable to more militant Communist nations.

(2) *Foreign States and their Agencies.* The question of the privileges and immunities granted under Soviet law to foreign states and their agencies is of obvious significance in evaluating proposals for adversary inspection. While Soviet legislation on civil procedure contains no specific provisions granting to foreign states or their agencies the right to sue in court, nevertheless such foreign state agencies might be considered to be foreign "organizations," and so have the right to judicial remedies granted by Article 59 of the USSR Fundamental Principles of Civil Procedure.[28] Article 59 gives to foreign enterprises and organizations the right to resort to Soviet courts and to exercise civil procedural rights for the defense of their interests. However, this paragraph of Article 59 must be compared with the paragraph of the same Article dealing not with foreign enterprises and organizations but with foreign citizens (i.e., individuals). The latter are given the right to resort to Soviet courts and to exercise civil procedural rights "equally with Soviet citizens." The distinction between the two paragraphs suggests that the rights of foreign enterprises and organizations are to be regulated by special rules. It is also to be noted that the third para-

---

28. Osnovy grazhdanskogo sudoproizvodstva Soiuza SSR i Soiuznykh Respublik, *Vedomosti*, 1961, no. 50, item 526; English translations: *CDSP*, Vol. XIV, no. 5 (February 28, 1962), pp. 3-9; *Soviet Civil Legislation and Procedure, Official Texts and Commentaries* (Moscow, [1964?]), pp. 146-175; University of Leyden, *Law in Eastern Europe*, no. 7, (Leyden, 1963), pp. 299-317. See L. A. Lunts, *Mezhdunarodnoe chastnoe pravo, osobennaia chast' {Private International Law, Special Part}* (Moscow, 1963), pp. 42-71. Relevant articles are printed in the Documentation, *infra* p. 105.

graph of Article 59 empowers the Council of Ministers of the USSR to establish retaliatory restrictions with respect to citizens, enterprises, and organizations of states which permit special limitations of the civil procedural rights of Soviet citizens, enterprises and organzations.

In order fully to safeguard an inspection agreement, it would be necessary to grant to foreign states the right to sue in Soviet courts and to clarify the rights of their agencies to sue, perhaps by treaty provisions similar to Article I, Section 1, of the Convention on the Privileges and Immunities of the United Nations or Article I of the Convention on the Legal Capacity, Privileges and Immunities of the Council for Mutual Economic Assistance.

The immunity of foreign states from suit is recognized by Article 61 of the USSR Fundamental Principles of Civil Procedure, which (a) requires the consent of the foreign state before suit is brought against it or its property in the USSR, (b) subjects diplomatic representatives of foreign states accredited in the USSR to the civil jurisdiction of a Soviet court "only within the limits established by the norms of international law or by agreements with the respective states," and (c) permits retaliatory measures to be imposed by the USSR Council of Ministers against a foreign state (or its property or its representatives) which does not grant the Soviet state (or its property or its representatives) the same judicial immunity as is granted to the foreign state under Article 61.

We shall discuss later the possibility of waiver of this immunity, so as to allow Soviet citizens and organizations to recover compensation for harm caused by a foreign inspection agency in the course of its operation.[29]

It is only in the area of diplomatic, consular, and trade representation that we find a highly developed body of Soviet legal practice with respect to the status of agencies of foreign states in the Soviet Union. The basic rules governing the status of these types of foreign state agencies are contained in the 1966 Statute on Diplomatic and Consular Representations[30] and in a number of bilateral international agreements.[31] Thus, for instance, the 1966 statute provides that diplomatic representatives shall enjoy personal immunity, freedom of communication with their own government,

---

29. See infra, pp. 43-44.
30. Printed in the Documentation, *infra* p. 116.
31. Listed in Jan F. Triska and Robert M. Slusser, *The Theory, Law, and Policy of Soviet Treaties* (Stanford, 1962), pp. 578-581; I. P. Blishchenko and V. N. Durdenevskii, *Diplomaticheskoe i konsul'skoe pravo {Diplomatic and Consular Law}* (Moscow, 1962), pp. 27-28; V. M. Shurshalov, general editor, *Mezhdunarodnopravovye formy sotrudnichestva sotsialisticheskikh gosudarstv {International Law Forms of Collaboration of Socialist States)* (Moscow, 1962), pp. 187-206. On the United States experience, see Donald G. Bishop, *The Roosevelt-Litvinov Agreements* (Syracuse, 1965).

and various other privileges. An example of the bilateral agreements is the still unratified US-USSR Consular Convention,[32] which lists in great detail the rights of a consular officer in protecting and assisting nationals of his state, and enumerates the rights, privileges, and immunities of consular officers, including some immunities (such as immunity from criminal jurisdiction) that are not provided by the 1966 Statute or the norms of public international law. While Soviet authors claim that the Soviet Union grants to diplomatic, consular, and trade agencies all those privileges and immunities that international law requires,[33] actual Soviet practice often places a highly restrictive interpretation upon the privileges and immunities of embassies, consulates, and trade delegations. This practice is exemplified by the numerous restraints placed upon the staff of the United States Embassy in Moscow with respect to travel, photography, and other activities.

In addition to the more traditional forms of activity of foreign state agencies, the USSR, since 1959, has been host to many foreign governmental exhibitions of various types. In particular, the United States has sponsored a variety of industrial and cultural exhibitions in various Soviet cities. The legal and practical problems encountered in the operation of these exhibitions can help to locate pitfalls to be avoided in a disarmament inspection arrangement. These problems include difficulties encountered in importation of large quantities of goods under customs bond, the exercise of functions of a politically sensitive nature by foreign personnel without diplomatic immunity, and the hiring of Soviet laborers.

(3) *Diplomats.* Soviet law and practice adhere fairly closely to traditional international law standards of diplomatic immunity. The right to immunity is incorporated in Article 4 of the USSR Fundamental Principles of Criminal Legislation,[34] which provides that the criminal responsibility of foreign

---

32. Printed in the Documentation, *infra* p. 125. See S. Houston Lay, "The United States-Soviet Consular Convention," American Journal of International Law, Vol. 50 (1965) p. 876.

33. See Blishchenko and Durdenevskii, *supra* note 31, *passim.*

34. Osnovy ugolovnogo zakonodatel'stva Soiuza SSR i soiuznykh respublik, *Vedomosti,* 1959, no. 1, item 6; no. 7, item 60, as amended, *id.,* 1960, no. 19, item 207, no. 21, item 222, no. 27, item 291, no. 50, item 511-512; *id.,* 1962, no. 14, item 147, no. 17, item 178; *id.,* 1964, no. 20, item 244. English translations: CDSP, Vol. XI, no. 5, (March 4, 1959), pp. 7-11; *Fundamental Principles of Soviet Criminal Legislation, the Judicial System and Criminal Court Procedures; Official Texts and Commentaries* (Moscow, 1960), pp. 5-27; University of Leyden, *Law in Eastern Europe,* Vol. 3 (Leyden, 195), pp. 37-51. The standard Soviet commentary is V. D. Men'shagin and P. S. Romashkin, general editors, *Nauchno-prakticheskii kommentarii k osnovam ugolovnogo zakonodatel'stva Soiuza SSR i soiuznykh Respublik [A Scholarly and Practical Commentary to the Fundamental Principles*

diplomats who commit crimes on the territory of the USSR shall be decided by diplomatic means, and in the 1966 Statute.[35]

As we have seen, foreign diplomats are also accorded a broad civil immunity under Soviet law.

It is significant that with respect both to criminal and civil liability, the relevant provisions grant immunity not only to diplomatic representatives of foreign states but also to "other persons specified in appropriate laws and international agreements" (Article 61 of the Fundamental Principles of Civil Procedure) or "other citizens who, in accordance with prevailing laws and international agreements, are not subject to criminal jurisdiction in Soviet judicial institutions." Thus any immunity granted to disarmament inspectors by treaty would automatically be incorporated in Soviet domestic law.

However, it should be noted that under both Soviet and international law, the grant of diplomatic immunity does not relieve the recipient of the obligation to obey the laws of the country to which he is accredited. Article

---

of Criminal Legislation of the USSR and the Union Republics} (2nd ed., Moscow, 1961). The Fundamental Principles of Criminal Legislation are incorporated in the "General Part" of the criminal codes of the various repuublics. In particular, Articles 1-57 of the Criminal Code of the RSFSR (see *infra* p. 86) incorporate them almost verbatim. The Criminal Code of the RSFSR is translated and discussed in Berman and Spindler, *supra* note 5.

35. The 1966 Statute on Diplomatic and Consular Representations of Foreign States on the Territory of the USSR (printed in the Documentation, p. 116) appeared after this book was in page proof. It was therefore impossible to incorporate extensive references to the statute in the text.

The new statute differs in a number of respects from the 1927 Statute (Sobranie Zakonov SSSR [Collection of Laws of the USSR], 1927, no. 5, item 48) which it replaces. Many of its provisions reflect those of the 1961 Vienna Convention on Diplomatic Relations (see below, note 36). The new statute retains the traditionally broad scope of diplomatic immunity, while significantly adding to the range of consular privileges and immunities. Consular immunities, however, remain considerably fewer than those granted in the draft US-USSR Consular Convention (printed in the Documentation, p. 125).

A number of specific provisions of the statute have a direct bearing upon points discussed in the text of this book. In connection with the discussion in pages 18-19 of the text, one should consider the obligation imposed upon all those enjoying the privileges and immunities granted by the statute to obey Soviet laws (Article 2). In connection with the discussion of communications on page 29 of the text, one should consider the liberal terms of Article 9 of the Convention with respect to diplomatic couriers, and its highly restrictive provisions with respect to the use of radio transmitters. In connection with the discussion of compensation for damage to Soviet citizens on pages 43-44, one should consider the provision of Article 25 of the Convention that consular officials shall be liable for damage caused by traffic accidents even when traveling on official business.

For a Soviet commentary on the new Statute, see O. Khlestov, "Novoe Polozhenie ob inostrannykh diplomaticheskikh i konsulskikh predstavitel'stvakh" [The New Statute on Foreign Diplomatic and Consular Representations], *Sovetskoe gosudarstvc i pravo {Soviet State and Law}*, 1966, no. 8, p. 30.

41, Section 1, of the Vienna Convention on Diplomatic Relations[36] provides:

> Without prejudice to their privileges and immunities, it is the duty of all persons enjoying such privileges and immunities to respect the laws and regulations of the receiving state. They also have a duty not to interfere in the internal affairs of that state.

Moreover, if a diplomat "conspires against the receiving state and the conspiracy can be rendered harmless only by putting him in restraint, he may be arrested for the time being."[37] The leading Soviet treatise on diplomatic and consular law states:[38]

> . . . Measures amounting to direct compulsion should not be applied to a diplomat. However this principle does not exclude measures of self-defense, [or] the application of other measures in exceptional circumstances, directed at the prevention of the commission of a crime by the diplomatic agent.

Later the same treatise adds, "When a crime of a flagrant nature is committed by a diplomatic agent, practice allows the arrest and expulsion of the diplomatic agent by the government of the country in which he is present."[39]

It should also be kept in mind that a diplomat may be declared *persona non grata* at the sole discretion of the receiving state,[40] a discretion which has often been used by the Soviet government (as well as by other governments) to secure the withdrawal of diplomats accused of gathering precisely the types of information which the inspectors might seek to obtain. It seems

36. Signed at Vienna, April 18, 1961, U. N. Doc. A/CONF. 20/13, April 16, 1961, text printed in *American Journal of International Law,* Vol. 55, pp. 1064-1077, ratified by the USSR, *Vedomosti,* 1964, No. 8, item 97. As of June 1, 1966, the Convention has not been ratified by the US; however its provisions generally reflect the rules of customary international law.
37. H. Lauterpacht, editor, L. Oppenheim, *International Law,* Vol. I, *Peace* (8th ed., New York, 1955), pp. 790-791.
38. I. P. Blishchenko and V. N. Durdenevskii, *supra* note 31, p. 352.
39. *Id.,* at p. 358.
40. The Vienna Convention, *supra* note 36, Article 9, provides:
    1. The receiving state may at any time and without having to explain its decision, notify the sending state that the head of the mission or any member of the diplomatic staff of the mission is *persona non grata* or that any other member of the staff of the mission is not acceptable. In any such case, the sending state shall, as appropriate, either recall the person concerned or terminate his functions with the mission. A person may be declared *non grata* or not acceptable before arriving in the territory of the receiving state.
    2. If the sending state refuses or fails within a reasonable period to carry out its obligations under paragraph 1 of this article, the receiving state may refuse to recognize the person concerned as a member of the mission.

clear, therefore, that the immunities granted to the inspectors may need to be significantly greater than those ordinarily granted to foreign diplomats by international law or by Soviet practice.

The privileges (as distinct from the immunities) of the inspectors may likewise need to be considerably broader than those granted in Soviet practice to diplomats, whose activities are subject to many restrictions. Details of these Soviet restrictions, particularly with respect to travel, will be discussed in later sections of this study.

(4) *Aliens and Stateless Persons.* Except as otherwise provided by international law or agreement, inspectors who are not Soviet citizens are subject to the provisions of Soviet law dealing with the legal status of aliens. With some important exceptions Soviet law provides for identical legal treatment of aliens and Soviet citizens.[41] Thus Article 4 of the USSR Fundamental Principles of Criminal Legislation provides: "All persons who commit crimes on the territory of the USSR shall be held responsible in accordance with the laws in force at the place of the commission of the crimes . . ." The territory of the USSR is interpreted by two leading Soviet commentators to include: [42]

> The land territory within the bounds of the state borders, the internal water areas within the bounds of the state borders (internal seas, lakes, rivers, and canals), the so-called coastal (territorial) waters within the bounds of a twelve-mile belt, the air space over the land and water territories of the USSR, the war and merchant ships (vessels) under the flags of the USSR and the airships (airplanes) with the identifying markings of the USSR.

Article 5 of the same Fundamental Principles makes Soviet citizens and stateless persons, but not citizens of foreign states, criminally liable for violations of Soviet law committed outside Soviet territory.

A standard of equal treatment for foreign citizens under Soviet civil procedure is provided in Article 59 of the USSR Fundamental Principles of Civil Procedure, discussed earlier. A more qualified equality is granted in substantive civil law by Article 22 of the USSR Fundamental Principles of Civil Legislation, which states that foreign citizens shall have civil legal capacity on a basis of equality with Soviet citizens, but adds that "specific exceptions may be established by Legislation of the USSR." Article 22 also authorizes the Council of Ministers of the USSR to establish retaliatory

---

41. See the works by Boguslavsky and Rubanov on the legal position of aliens in the USSR, cited in the Bibliography; cf. Lunts, *supra,* note 28, *passim.*
42. Men'shagin and Romashkin, *supra* note 34, p. 17.

restrictions with respect to the citizens of those states in which there are special restrictions upon the civil legal capacity of Soviet citizens.

Article 129 of the Fundamental Principles of Civil Legislation and Article 64 of the Fundamental Principles of Civil Procedure Legislation provide that where rules established by international treaty or agreement conflict with Soviet federal or republican statute law in civil matters, the rules established by the treaty or agreement shall be applied. Similarly Article 4 of the Fundamental Principles of Criminal Legislation provides for the automatic application of treaty provisions exempting aliens from criminal liability. Thus in these areas, as in the area of diplomatic immunities, special privileges given to aliens by treaty would be incorporated automatically into Soviet law. Similar "automatic incorporation" clauses are not found, however, in Soviet criminal procedure legislation. If it were desired to give inspectors special privileges in criminal proceedings without entirely exempting them from criminal jurisdiction, it would be important to have specific references to these privileges incorporated in Soviet criminal procedure legislation.

We may conclude, from this brief survey, that under Soviet law aliens are, in general, accorded a status equivalent to that of Soviet citizens; to use the terminology of international law, they are accorded "national treatment." This fact alone, however, would by no means assure to foreign inspectors on Soviet soil the legal guarantees necessary to the carrying out of their functions, for, as will be discussed in detail below, Soviet law places important restrictions on the rights of Soviet citizens to travel and to have access to information.

In addition, there are many specific exceptions to the rule of national treatment in Soviet law and practice. Some, such as the denial to aliens of the right to vote, would be of no significance to alien inspectors; others, such as the Soviet practice of creating administrative obstacles to marriage between Soviet citizens and aliens, might conceivably create some friction; still others, such as Soviet restrictions upon freedom of travel by aliens, might prevent inspectors from performing their verification functions. The last type of restriction will be discussed in some detail in later sections of this study.

B. SPECIFIC PRIVILEGES AND IMMUNITIES NEEDED BY THE INSPECTORATE

(1) *Entry into and Exit from the Soviet Union.* The Statute on Entry

21

into the USSR and Exit from the USSR[43] gives the Ministry of Foreign Affairs and certain other Soviet state agencies complete discretion in the granting or denial of permission to enter or leave the Soviet Union. Refusal of such permission would be considered an administrative matter and would not be subject to judicial review. However, the Procuracy of the USSR would have the power to protest to higher agencies, up to the Council of Ministers of the USSR, abuses of discretion by subordinate officials, and also the power to prosecute such officials for abuse or neglect of their official duties.[44]

If an inspector were to attempt to cross the Soviet border without appropriate permission, he would violate Article 20 of the Law on State Crimes,[45] which punishes "Unlawful Departure Abroad and Unlawful Entry Into the USSR." If an inspector should attempt to fly over the Soviet border without appropriate permission, or if by carelessness he crossed the border at the wrong point, he would violate Article 21 of the Law on State Crimes, "Violation of the Rules of International Flights."[46]

In the light of these existing restriction, it seems clear that a treaty or agreement providing for inspection in the Soviet Union, if it is effectively to secure freedom of entry and departure by inspectors across Soviet borders, should require (a) an exemption from the requirements of permission of the Ministry of Foreign Affairs or other Soviet state agencies; (b) the amendment of the Statute on Entry into the USSR and Exit from the USSR to give inspectors the right to enter and depart without permission; (c) the amendment of the Statute on the Procuracy to require the Procuracy to protest refusals of Soviet officials to permit entry or exit of inspectors; and (d) the enactment of an all-union statute making it a crime to obstruct the entry or exit of inspectors.

---

43. Polozhenie o v"ezde v Soiuz Sovetskikh Sotsialisticheskikh Respublik i o vyezde iz Soiuza Sovetskikh Sotsialisticheskikh Respublik [Statute on Entry into the USSR and Exit from the USSR], SP SSSR, 1959, no. 13, item 80, published in *Sbornik normativnykh materialov po voprosam vneshnei torgovli SSSR, Vypusk 1 {Collection of Normative Materials on the Foreign Trade of the USSR, Issue 1}* (Moscow, 1961), p. 272.
44. Statute on Procuratorial Supervision in the USSR, *supra* note 5, Chapters I and II.
45. Zakon ob ugolovnoi otvetstvennosti za gosudarstvennye prostupleniia, *Vedomosti,* 1959, no. 1, item 8. This law has been amended a number of times. The current version is the same as Articles 64-88-2 of the Criminal Code of the RSFSR; translated in the Documentation, *infra* p. 89. The standard Soviet commentary is V. D. Men'shagin and B. A. Kurinov, *Nauchno-prakticheskii kommentarii k zakonu ob ugolovnoi otvetstvennosti za gosudarstvennye prestupleniia {Scholarly and Practical Commentary to the Law on Criminal Liability for Crimes Against the State}* (2nd rev. ed., Moscow, 1961).
46. Identical with Article 84 of the Criminal Code of the RSFSR, printed in the Documentation, *infra* p. 92.

(2) *Import and Export of Goods and Records.* In the course of performing its functions, an inspectorate would need to import and export various types of goods and records. In determining the legal arrangements necessary to facilitate such import and export, it could draw upon the experiences of foreign embassies and consulates in the Soviet Union, which, despite some difficulties, have arrived at workable arrangements with the Soviet government concerning diplomatic exemptions from customs requirements. However, the needs of an inspectorate might be both greater than and different from those of an embassy, particularly if, as is suggested below, it were thought necessary to ensure the independence of the inspectors from Soviet sources of supply.

At present the Customs Code provides that the import and export of goods by diplomatic and consular representations and international organizations shall be governed by administrative regulations issued jointly by the Ministries of Foreign Affairs, Foreign Trade, and Finances.[47] While Article 20 of the Customs Code provides for automatic application of treaty rules in customs matters, for the sake of clarity it might be necessary to amend the above-mentioned regulations to provide for those needs of the inspection organization that could not be met by imports and exports through the rather restrictive ordinary customs process, which involves, in many instances, very high tariffs and complicated clearance procedures.[48]

(3) *Housing, Food, and Services.* Most tangible property in the Soviet Union belongs to the state or to social organizations controlled by the state and by the Communist Party. Articles 4 through 11 of the Constitution provide for the socialist ownership and operation of all important means of production except for some small scale farming and handicrafts. Virtually all service organizations (transportation, communications, restaurants, hotels, *etc.*) are state enterprises. In practice this means that no foreigner can expect to live in the Soviet Union and carry on any type of activity without the active cooperation of many Soviet state organizations. Arrangements for apartments involve dealings with one state agency; for food with another; for transportation with a third; for the hiring of labor with a fourth; for financial transactions with a fifth. In a number of instances foreigners are compelled by law to deal with state agencies

47. Tamozhennyi kodeks Soiuza SSR [Customs Code of the USSR], *Vedomosti,* 1964, no. 20, item 242, Article 59.
48. See *Tamozhennyi tarif SSSR {Customs Tariff of the USSR}* (Moscow, 1962).

especially established to deal with foreigners; [49] in other instances foreigners voluntarily deal with such agencies rather than those open to the general public because the special service agencies for foreigners are generally much better equipped to supply the goods or services needed. These agencies often have a monopoly position which would enable them to charge arbitrary prices.

Thus an international inspectorate on Soviet territory could, if the Soviet government so desired, be subjected to harassment with respect to living arrangements and procurement of food and services. Presumably the Soviet government would not so desire, except as a signal of its intention to terminate an inspection agreement, or to show its displeasure at the manner in which the inspection agreement was being carried out. We have no proposals for changes in Soviet law to guarantee freedom from such harassment, but would only suggest that any inspection treaty or agreement should include a commitment by all governments concerned to facilitate in all possible ways the procurement of housing, food, and services by the inspectorate. If the inspectorate were unable to obtain needed goods locally, it could attempt to import them, and thus test the intention of Soviet authorities to force them to curtail inspection operations, with what-ever consequences the disarmament agreement may provide for such a contingency.

(4) *Freedom of Travel.* Soviet law places significant direct restrictions upon travel by foreigners with or without diplomatic status. These restrictions represent an integral part of the Soviet system of civil and military secrecy, and so it is unlikely that the Soviet government would be willing to abolish them, except possibly in the context of a disarmament agreement that made such secrecy unnecessary. If, however, the Soviet government did wish to abolish direct restrictions on travel by inspectors, it could easily do so and any re-imposition of such direct restrictions could easily be detected. A much more difficult technical problem is presented by the indirect restrictions on travel created by government ownership and control of all transportation facilities. To the extent that the inspectorate is forced to depend upon the public transportation system or charter Soviet-owned transportation, its freedom of movement will be subject to subtle indirect control.

---

49. American tourists, for instance, must usually pay Intourist, the Soviet state monopoly travel agency, in advance in dollars for all accommodations within the Soviet Union as a prerequisite to obtaining a Soviet visa. The legal status of Intourist is discussed in D. M. Genkin, general editor, *Pravovoe regulirovanie vneshnei torgovli SSSR {The Legal Regulation of the Foreign Trade of the USSR},* (Moscow, 1961), pp. 366-376.

Certain areas of the Soviet Union are closed to all persons not having special permission. The Statute on the Defense of the State Border of the USSR [50] provides for the establishment of closed zones along the borders of the USSR. Article 8 of the Statute provides:

> In the interests of the defense of the state border, the Council of Ministers of the USSR, or, by its authorization, the Councils of Ministers of the Union and Autonomous Republics, shall in necessary cases establish a border zone and a border belt on the land and water territory of the USSR.
>
> The border zone shall be established, as a rule within the boundaries of the territory of the district, city, rural or village Soviet of Working-People's Deputies adjacent to the state border. In the composition of a border zone, where one is established, shall be included also the territorial and internal sea waters of the USSR and the Soviet part of the waters of border rivers and lakes. Appropriate rules shall be in effect in the border zone.
>
> The width of a border belt should not exceed 2 km. from the line of the state border on dry land or from the banks of border rivers (or lakes). Within the limits of this belt, the border forces shall enforce additional restrictions.
>
> The Soviet part of the waters of border rivers and lakes, and also islands in these rivers and lakes belonging to the USSR, shall be under the exclusive supervision of the border forces.

Article 10 of the same Statute provides:

> Entrance within the limits of a border zone by persons who are not permanent residents of that zone shall be forbidden without the permission of agencies of the police, unless some other procedure is established.

> Entrance within the limits of a border belt and residence therein shall be allowed only with permission of the border forces.

The purpose of many of the border zones is probably the prevention of unauthorized travel abroad by Soviet citizens. Since entrance into border zones by inspectors would not jeopardize the accomplishment of this purpose, the Soviet Union might be willing to allow the inspectors to enter border zones on more liberal terms than its own citizens.

In addition to the border zones, certain other areas, presumably of mili-

---

50. Polozhenie ob okhrane gosudarstvennoi granitsy Soiuza Sovetskikh Sotsialisticheskikh Respublik, *Vedomosti*, 1960, no. 34, item 324.

tary significance, are closed both to foreigners and to Soviet citizens without special permission.[51] Also considerable areas of the Soviet Union are freely open to Soviet citizens but are closed to foreigners. In some instances foreigners are allowed to travel through these closed areas along prescribed routes; in others they are not. Even for travel to "open" areas, foreigners resident in the Soviet Union are required to have the specific permission of Soviet police agencies, a permission which is often refused. These travel restrctions are embodied in unpublished regulations; however, many of them have been transmitted to the American Embassy in Moscow through official channels.

It may be assumed that appropriate changes would be made in these laws and regulations to allow inspectors to travel freely within those areas of the Soviet Union that were opened to inspection. However, as mentioned above, a number of problems would remain. It would be necessary to clarify the question of the right of inspectors to purchase tickets directly from public carriers. At present foreigners are forced to deal on many travel matters through Intourist, the Soviet state travel agency for foreigners.[52] This requirement would subject the inspectors' travel arrangements to the control of an agency that has long been thought to perform surveillance and control functions as well as normal travel agency activities. Intourist is organized on a nation-wide basis, and it is the practice of local agencies to telephone Moscow for instructions whenever any unusual situation is encountered.[53] While Intourist does receive some preferences in booking travel reservations, it apparently does not ordinarily have the right to secure cancellation of reservations held by Soviet citizens in order to secure space for foreigners. An inspector who wishes to fly to a given city to conduct an inspection might be told by Intourist or the airline ticket office (if he was permitted to use the latter) that no more space was available. There would be no simple way to determine in such a case whether deliberate interference with the performance of inspection functions was taking place.

An alternative would be for the inspectorate to charter airplanes, helicopters, and automobiles in the Soviet Union. Since Soviet law forbids the

51. V. A. Vlasov, and S. S. Studenikin, *Sovetskoe administrativnoe pravo {Soviet Administrative Law}* (Moscow, 1959), p. 276.
52. See *supra* note 49.
53. The experience of the authors in this regard is confirmed by that of many other visitors to the Soviet Union with whom they have spoken.

operation of private means of transportation for hire,[54] the means of transportation would have to be chartered from a Soviet state agency. Again the inspectors would be dependent upon the active cooperation of the Soviet government in order to travel where they wished. If the Soviet charter agency reported that all its helicopters were out of order, the inspectors would have no easy means of verifying the truth of this statement or of learning if the helicopters had been deliberately disabled.

A second alternative would be for the inspectorate to use its own means of transportation and to have them under its complete physical control. Soviet legal practice recognizes the right of foreign individuals, organizations, and states to own movable property in accordance with generally recognized principles of private international law. Visits by foreign airplanes, ships, and automobiles for purposes of passenger and freight transportation and tourist travel are frequent.

Even though the inspection organization would then be free to own automobiles, airplanes, helicopters, boats, *etc.,* within the Soviet Union, severe legal restrictions might be encountered in their use. The Soviet Union, like all countries with modern transportation systems, has a complex body of highway traffic and air safety regulations. Both the United States and the USSR are parties to the 1949 Convention on Road Traffic.[55] The basic Soviet traffic regulations have been amended to conform to this

54. "The following private trades and the issuance of licenses for them are prohibited: . . . the transport of passengers and freight on automobiles, trucks and motorcycles." Pravila registratsii nekooperirovannykh kustarei [Rules of Registration of Private Craftsmen], as amended through April 22, 1958, printed in *Grazhdanskii kodeks RSFSR {Civil Code of the RSFSR}* (Moscow, 1961), pp. 166-173. Administrative and criminal sanctions are provided for violations of these rules. Cf. Criminal Code of the RSFSR, Article 162, printed in the Documentation, *infra* p. 95. Soviet citizens are not allowed in practice to own aircraft. This practice is reflected in the fact that no provision is made in the Soviet Air Code for registration of privately owned aircraft. Vozdushnyi kodeks Soiuza SSR [Air Code of the USSR], *Vedomosti,* 1961, no. 52, item 538, Article 10.

55. Signed September 19, 1949, 3 UST and OIA 3008; TIAS no. 2487; 125 UNTS 22. The Soviet Union has made the following reservation to this treaty: "The Government of the Union of Soviet Socialist Republics does not consider itself bound by the provisions of Article 33 of the Convention on Road Traffic, which lays down that disputes between Contracting States concerning the interpretation or application of this Convention may be referred to the International Court of Justice for decision by application from any of the States concerned, and declares that the agreement of all the States in dispute is required in each separate case for the submission of any dispute to the International Court of Justice for decision." [Translation by the United Nations Secretariat.] The Government of the United States has informed the United Nations Secretary-General that it has no objection to this reservation, but "considers that it may and hereby states that it will apply this reservation reciprocally with respect to the Soviet Union."

convention.[56] The convention, however, specifies only the most general rules of the road, leaving most matters to the jurisdiction of the signatory states. The USSR is not a party to the Chicago Convention on International Civil Aviation,[57] but many provisions of the Soviet Air Code of 1961[58] are in accord with the principles of that convention. The Air Code contains only the general outlines of Soviet air law and is supplemented by regulations issued by the Chief Administration of the Civil Air Fleet, its successor, the Ministry of Civil Aviation of the USSR,[59] and other Soviet government agencies.[60] It may be assumed that the inspectors would wish to obey these traffic and air travel regulations whenever they could do so without impeding their inspection mission. In view of the difficulty of securing copies of these regulations,[61] it might be necessary to secure a Soviet commitment to supply copies of the regulations and all amendments thereto. A quotation of two of the articles of the Soviet Air Code may serve to illustrate the type of problem that could be encountered:

> Article 52. Every flight of an aircraft must be made in accordance with a flight plan approved in the prescribed manner. Deviation from the flight plan is allowed only with permission of the traffic control service.
>
> All instructions of the traffic control service are compulsory for the crews of aircraft and must be unquestioningly obeyed by them. However, in case of a clear danger to the safety of flight, the commander of the aircraft may, depending upon the circumstances that have arisen, make an independent decision involving a deviation from the flight plan and instructions of the traffic control. The commander of the aircraft must immediately inform the traffic control service of the decision he has taken.
>
> Article 53. Flights by aircraft may be made only under appropriate weather conditions. . . .

56. Izvestia, December 4, 1963, p. 4, col. 1.*Pravila dvizheniia po ulitsam gorodov, naselennykh punktov i dorogam SSSR* (*Regulations for Traffic on City and Town Streets and the Roads of the USSR)* (Gorky, 1964). The regulations were long unavailable even within the USSR. Cf. Izvestia, May 17, 1964, p. 5, cols. 1-5. There are many secondary traffic rules, *e.g.,* Pravila proezda avtoguzhevogo transporta cherez pereezdy zheleznvhk dorog, utverzhdennve Ministerstvom putei soobschcheniia SSR [Rules of Crossing Railroad Tracks by Haulage Trucking, approved by the Ministry of Railroads of the USSR], mentioned in Soviet publications, but unavailable outside the USSR.
57. Convention on International Civil Aviation, December 7, 1944, 61 Stat. 1180, TIAS no. 1591; 15 UNTS 295.
58. *Supra* note 54. See Dennis A. Cooper, *The Air Code of the USSR* (Translated and Annotated) (Charlottesville, Va., 1966).
59. *Vedomosti,* 1964, no. 31, item 373.
60. Air Code, *supra* note 54, Articles 6, 69, 119. These regulations are not generally available outside the USSR.
61. *Supra* notes 56 and 60.

While it is easy to envision violations of automobile speed limits or parking restrictions by an inspector in order to perform his duties, it is doubtful that it would be technically possible to give an airplane, even one belonging to the inspectorate, the right to land at a crowded Soviet airport despite a warning by the Soviet air traffic controller that the runway was not clear.

If it were sought, as part of an inspection arrangement, to secure freedom of travel for the inspectorate, it would be necessary not only to secure the repeal of specific Soviet restrictions upon travel by foreigners and immunity from certain Soviet traffic regulations, but also to provide the inspectors with physical control of their means of transportation. For the travel provisions to be acceptable it would be necessary to avoid undue interference with the Soviet transportation system. This might be done (a) by the provision of facilities and equipment independent of the Soviet transportation system, such as airports controlled by the inspectorate and long-range helicopters or VTOL planes and (b) by requiring notification of intended travel.

(5) *Communications.* To the extent that the inspection organization relied upon the Soviet public communications network, it would face problems of total Soviet state control analogous to those mentioned above with respect to travel. The use of diplomatic pouches and leased teletype facilities similar to those used by the American Embassy in Moscow might satisfy some of its needs for rapid and confidential communication; however, for emergencies it would appear to need, in addition, the right to maintain its own short-wave transmitters and receivers. Unlicensed operation of radio transmitters is prohibited by Soviet law.[62]

---

62. *E.g.,* a Russian Republic decree of April 7, 1960, provides: "The Presidium of the Supreme Soviet of the RSFSR *decrees:*

"1. That the construction and use of radio transmitting apparatus without appropriate permission shall result in the application of measures of social pressure or measures of administrative pressure in the form of a fine in the amount of five hundred rubles, [the sum is expressed in pre-1961 rubles. Five hundred such "old" rubles would be equal to fifty of the rubles now in circulation or $55.56 at the official rate of exchange.—Authors' note] with the confiscation of the radio apparatus used.

"2. Materials on illegal preparation and use of radio transmitting apparatus shall be heard by people's judges sitting individually within three days from the receipt of the materials by the court from the police. The person who committed the violation, and, where necessary, witnesses shall be summoned.

"The decree of a people's judge imposing a fine shall be executed immediately and shall not be subject to appeal.

"3. A decree of a people's judge adjudging guilt of illegal construction and use of radio transmitting apparatus can be reversed or altered on the protest of a procurator by the same people's judge, or by the chairman of the appropriate area (or national area), regional, territorial court, court of an autonomous region, or Supreme Court of an autonomous republic." *RSFSR Vedomosti,* 1960, no. 13, item 177.

It would be necessary therefore to obtain either exemption from the licensing requirement or a Soviet commitment to provide the necessary licenses.

(6) *Gathering of Information.* Under the present Soviet law, almost any action an inspector might wish to take would be a violation of Article 2 of the Law on Criminal Responsibility for Crimes Against the State, on espionage.[63] According to this article, espionage consists of either (a) transfer or the stealing or collection for the purpose of transfer to a foreign state or foreign organization of information constituting a state or military secret, or (b) transfer or collection on assignment from a foreign intelligence service of any other information for use to the detriment of the interests of the USSR. Whether or not the acts of the inspectorate would fall under the second clause might be debatable; however it is clear that the inspectorate's actions would fall under the first clause, insofar as the information gathered by the inspectorate was subject to state or military secrecy. In view of the extremely broad definition given to state and military secrets in Soviet law,[63a] it seems likely that most of the information the inspectorate would want to gather would fall into one of these categories.

Soviet law also places severe restrictions upon photography both from the air and on the ground. Article 57 of the Soviet Air Code provides:

> Photography, cinematography and the use of radio communication apparatus on board an aircraft is permitted in accordance with the procedure defined by special rules established by the Chief Administration of the Civil Air Fleet attached to the Council of Ministers of the USSR with the agreement of interested Ministries and Departments.

These rules prohibit photography from the air by foreigners. Severe restrictions also apply to the photographing of border areas and military or transportation facilities. The Soviet Ministry of Foreign Affairs has informed the American Embassy in Moscow, by notes delivered from time to time, of further restrictions upon photography by foreigners.[64] Soviet

---

63. Identical with Article 64 of the Criminal Code of the RSFSR, printed in the Documentation, *infra* p. 89.
63a. See discussion *infra,* pp. 34-36.
64. A Soviet guidebook gives the following "Rules for Taking Photographs:"
   "In the USSR, as in other countries, it is prohibited to photograph, film or sketch military facilities, railway and highway bridges, hydrotechnical installations (sluices, dams, pumping stations), railway junctions, tunnnels, industrial enterprises, research institutions, designing offices and laboratories, power stations, radio towers and radio-telephone and telegraph stations. It is also prohibited to photograph and film the ground from aircraft.
   "If the visitor wants to photograph or film an interior (museums, office buildings, factories, *etc.*) he must have the permission of the administration." V. Chernov and V. Mazov, *Moscow, a Tourist's Guide* (Moscow, [1962?]), p. 195.

citizens are well aware of restrictions upon photography by foreigners. Embassy personnel and tourists have often been detained while taking photographs by groups of private citizens (who in some instances may have been encouraged in this by Soviet authorities). Thus if the inspectors were to engage in photography, it would be necessary not only to change the law but also to make the changes plain to the Soviet public.

(7) *Wiretapping and Electronic Eavesdropping.* There appear to be no constitutional or statutory restrictions upon wiretapping or electronic eavesdropping in the USSR when done by Soviet authorities. However, inspectors wishing to wiretap or eavesdrop would need to enter upon government property and might need the cooperation of Soviet communications agencies. Again, it would be important to provide for this not only in any treaty but also in Soviet legislation and in administrative regulatons.

(8) *Legal Protection of the Inspectorate.* It would appear that Soviet law, as it now reads, would provide considerable legal protection to the personnel of the inspectorate. The regular provisions of Soviet criminal law provide for punishment of homicide, assault and battery, theft, fraud, and other crimes against the life, health, freedom, and dignity of the person and against personal property; and these penalties apply equally whether or not the victim is a Soviet citizen.[65] In addition, Article 4 of the Law on State Crimes [66] provides extremely severe punishment — deprivation of freedom for a term of ten to fifteen years with confiscation of property, with or without additional exile for two to five years, or death with confiscation of property — for the assassination of or infliction of severe bodily injury upon a representative of a foreign state with the goal of provoking war or international complications. It would seem that this article would apply to any attack upon a disarmament inspector who was a "representative of a foreign state." The Soviet government should be willing to amend the article to cover in addition representatives of an international organization.

It is not so clear that property belonging to a foreign government or

---

65. *Ugolovnyi kodeks RSFSR: Ofitsial'nyi tekst s izmeneniiami na* 1 *dekabria* 1963 *g., i s prilozheniem postateino-sistematizerovannykh materialov {Criminal Code of the RSFSR, Official Text with Amendments as of December* 1, 1963 *and with Appendix of Materials Arranged by Articles}* (Moscow, 1964). The Code, as amended to July 3, 1965, is translated and discussed in Berman and Spindler, *supra* note 5. The standard but unofficial Soviet commentary is B. S. Nikiforov, general editor, *Nauchno-prakticheskii kommentarii k ugolovnomy kodeksy RSFSR {A Scholarly and Practical Commentary to the Criminal Code of the RSFSR}* (2nd ed., Moscow, 1964). Relevant articles of the code are printed in the Documentation, *infra* p. 86.
66. Identical with Article 67 of the Criminal Code of the RSFSR, printed in the Documentation, *infra* p. 89.

international inspection organization would be protected under Soviet criminal law. Article 101 of the Criminal Code of the Russian Republic provides that crimes against the property of "other socialist states" shall be punished according to the law of crimes against the property of the Soviet state; however, protection of the property of a non-socialist state or of an international inspection organization is provided, if at all, only under Article 151 of the same code, which makes crimes against the property of associations that are not socialist organizations punishable according to the law of crimes against the personal property of citizens. According to an authoritative but unofficial Soviet commentary the word associations here includes those of foreign "capitalist" states.[67] However, the commentary does not discuss the protection of the property of international organizations. In addition, the penalties for crimes against the personal property of citizens are relatively mild. It would seem desirable, therefore, that any disarmament agreement providing for inspection should require Soviet law to be amended to provide expressly that crimes against the property of the inspectorate be punished on the same terms as crimes against Soviet state property.

As mentioned above, the individual members of the verification organization would have the right to resort to the Soviet courts for the vindication of their civil law rights. However, the right of foreign governments and international organizations to sue in Soviet courts is not clearly stated in Soviet law. For the sake of certainty, it would be desirable to define this right by international agreement, as has already been done in the case of the United Nations.[68]

It is not clear, moreover, that a foreigner or foreign organization or government has the same rights as a Soviet citizen to complain to the procuracy about administrative abuses or about erroneous judicial decisions, and to have such complaints investigated and acted upon. The relevant statute provides only for the processing of complaints by "citizens."[69] Unless this statute were amended, the inspectors might not have access to one of the basic Soviet channels for the vindication of legal rights.

67. Nikiforov, *supra* note 65, at p. 319.
68. Convention on Privileges and Immunities of the United Nations, Documentation, *infra* p. 140, Section 1 (c).
69. Statute on Procuratorial Supervision in the USSR, *supra* note 5, Article 14.

III.

LEGAL PROBLEMS
CONNECTED WITH THE PERFORMANCE
OF INSPECTION FUNCTIONS

A. INSPECTION OF PROPERTY AND DOCUMENTS BELONGING TO THE SOVIET STATE

The vast majority of the things in the Soviet Union which might be subject to inspection under a disarmament agreement are state-owned, as can be seen from the language of Article 6 of the Soviet Constitution. Under present Soviet law, entry by inspectors upon much of this state-owned property would be prevented (1) by administrative regulations limiting access to those on officially approved business and (2) by secrecy laws and regulations.

Factories, military installations, *etc.*, while legally considered property of the Soviet state as a whole, are assigned in accordance with Soviet law to the "operative administration" of various state agencies.[70] These agencies, in exercising their right and duty of "operative administration," exercise many of the rights traditionally associated with property ownership. In particular, they can and do exclude the general public from their premises. Many different systems of passes and identification documents are used by state agencies to allow the entry of authorized persons and to prevent the entry of unauthorized persons. It would seem necessary to provide the inspectors with some sort of pass that could be accepted by all the state agencies whose property they had a right to inspect. At the same time, it might be necessary to limit their powers so that their inspection would not be overly disruptive of the normal activities of these agencies. Considerable help in determining what powers the inspectors might need and what they might not need could be obtained by studying the powers

---

70. Fundamental Principles of Civil Legislation, *supra* note 18, Art. 21.

granted by the Soviet government to its own inspection and auditing agencies.[71]

A great many of the documents and materials which the inspectors might wish to see are classified as secret under present Soviet laws and administrative regulations. These laws and regulations serve a variety of purposes: preventing other countries from obtaining information about military technology or location of possible targets that could weaken Soviet military strength; preventing the disclosure of foreign trade plans, industrial secrets, and other information that would help economic competitors of the Soviet Union; preventing the disclosure of information embarrassing to the Soviet regime or to private Soviet citizens. To the extent that a disarmament arrangement enhanced Soviet security, the Soviet leadership might be willing to expose some of its military secrets to the inspectorate. However any inspection arrangement that infringed unduly upon the other purposes of Soviet secrecy legislation might be unacceptable to Soviet negotiators. It would therefore seem worthwhile to conduct a close analysis of the scope of Soviet secrecy regulations and practices, in order to evaluate the extent to which a given inspection arrangement might infringe upon Soviet secrecy interests.

Soviet secrecy legislation provides for two classification systems: one is for the purpose of determining the type of handling to be given to documents in accordance with the importance of the information they contain; the other is for the purpose of determining the penalty to be applied for improper disclosure or obtaining of secret information.[72] For purposes of precautions to be taken in handling, secret information is classified in a descending order of importance, as: top secret, secret, not to be made public, and for official use. For purposes of imposing penalties, documents are classified in a descending order of importance, as: state secrets of a military character, other state secrets, official secrets of a mili-

---

71. As of late 1964, there were 22 federal inspection agencies in the USSR, plus numerous republican and local inspection agencies. Ia. A. Zdir, "O roli gosudarstvennykh inspektsii v obespechenii sotsialisticheskoi zakonnosti v gosudarstvennom upravlenii" [The Role of State Inspection Agencies in the Securing of Socialist Legality in State Administration], *Sovetskoe gosudarstvo i pravo {Soviet State and Law}*, 1964, no. 11, p. 56. A detailed description of the functions and powers of a number of such agencies is given in Ia. A. Zdir, *Gosudarstvennye inspektsii v SSSR {State Inspection Agencies in the USSR}* (Moscow 1960). The charter of the Committee of Party and State Control, the most important of the inspection agencies during the early 1960's, is translated in the Documentation, *infra* p. 63. A brief survey of the functions and powers of other law enforcement agencies is given in A. E. Lunev, *Obespechenie zakonnosti v sovetskom gosudarstvennom upravlenii {Securing Legality in Soviet State Administration}* (Moscow, 1963).
72. Peter Maggs, "Der nichtmilitärischer Geheimschutz nach Sowjetrecht," *Osteuropa-Recht*, Vol. 11 (1965), p. 161.

tary character, and other official secrets. Thus transfer of a state or military secret to a foreign agent is punishable by death, while loss of a document containing non-military official secrets may involve only mild disciplinary penalties.

Since nearly all the information the inspectorate would wish to obtain would be of a military nature, it would be very highly classified under both systems of classification. The scope of state secrets, the highest classification grade for criminal law purposes, was significantly narrowed by a new list issued in 1956,[73] but the changes involved mainly information of a political and economic nature, while the list of state secrets of a military nature was kept substantially the same. Information on defense production was transferred to the heading of state secrets of an economic nature, a change without significant legal effect under present Soviet law. An examination of the present list of state secrets shows that it includes all kinds of information related to number of troops, amount of armaments, and military production capacities. Both the inspectors and the Soviet officials and citizens who cooperated with them would need some sort of exemption from the operation of the criminal penalties for the obtaining or revealing of such secrets. At the same time, it would be necessary to develop some legal sanctions that would restrict disclosure by inspectors of nonmilitary secrets accidentally discovered by them.

B. INTERROGATION OF SOVIET OFFICIALS

An edict of December 16, 1947,[74] places severe limitations upon co-operation by Soviet officials with representatives of foreign states. With certain exceptions, it provides that all officials, upon receiving an inquiry from a representative of a foreign state, must direct the inquirer to the Ministry of Foreign Affairs or the Ministry of Foreign Trade, and may not answer the inquiry directly. The only general exception to this rule is for state employees who must deal with representatives of foreign states in the course of the everyday life of the latter — in restaurants, stores, post offices, etc. This edict, enacted in a period of xenophobic distrust of foreigners, is still in force, although a number of exceptions are permitted in practice today, e.g., negotiations on cultural exchange by the Ministry of Higher and Specialized Secondary Education. While contact

---

73. Printed in the Documentation, *infra* p. 112. See generally George Ginsburgs and Armins Rusis, "Soviet Criminal Law and the Protection of State Secrets," in University of Leyden, *Law in Eastern Europe,* no. 7, (Leyden, 1963), pp. 3-48.
74. Printed in the Documentation, *infra* p. 114.

between Soviet officials and private foreign citizens is apparently not restricted by any published law or regulation, there are in practice limitations on the channels through which even such contact is allowed. It would be necessary to consider whether an inspectorate could operate effectively if it had to channel its questions to Soviet officials through a ministry in Moscow, and, if not, what broader powers would be acceptable to the Soviet government.

A second problem concerns the scope of the questions that Soviet officials may be permitted to answer. This problem is illustrated by the restrictions in Soviet law concerning the execution of letters rogatory (commissions to Soviet courts by foreign courts). On November 22, 1935, the United States and the Soviet Union exchanged notes constituting an agreement relating to the procedure to be followed in the execution of letters rogatory.[75] Paragraph 8 of the Soviet note reserves the right not to execute letters rogatory calling for answers to questions that might infringe upon the "safety or security" of the USSR. A similar limitation is contained in Article 62 of the Fundamental Principles of Civil Procedure, which provides that Soviet courts shall execute commissions of foreign judicial agencies, relating to the effectuation of specific procedural acts (the service of writs and other documents, the questioning of parties and witnesses, the effectuation of expert studies and viewings, *etc.*) with the exception of cases when: (1) the execution of the commission would contradict the sovereignty of the USSR or would threaten its security, and (2) the execution of the commission is not within the competence of the courts.

In view of the fact that present Soviet secrecy laws bar Soviet officials from revealing many types of information that the inspectors might need to obtain, it would probably be necessary for the inspection arrangement (1) to provide for the declassification of certain types of information or of all documents contained in a given zone or (2) to authorize Soviet officials to give such information to inspectors without being liable to the severe criminal and disciplinary penalties now imposed for the revelation of classified information.[76]

Finally, problems might arise concerning the procedures for and methods of questioning used by the inspectorate. The inspection agreement could

---

75. Printed in the Documentation, *infra* p. 120.
76. See Articles 1, 12, and 13 of the Law on Criminal Responsibility for Crimes Against the State, identical with Articles 64, 75, and 76, respectively, of the Criminal Code of the RSFSR, Documentation, *infra* p. 91.; Ginsburgs and Rusis, *supra* note 73; Maggs, *supra* note 72; Article 23 of the Law on Military Crimes, identical with Article 259 of the Criminal Code of the RSFSR, Documentation, *infra* p. 103.

provide that Soviet authorities would order government officials and military officials and military personnel to answer questions put by the inspectors. For failure to answer, the Soviet officials and military personnel would then be subject to the penalties provided by Soviet criminal, administrative, labor, and military law for failure to obey the order of a superior. Alternatively, violation of the disarmament agreement could be made a crime, and the inspectorate could be given the investigatory powers assigned to an "agency of inquiry" by the codes of criminal procedure. Problems of the latter procedure will be discussed in detail below in the section on "Interrogation of Private Soviet Citizens."

C. DIRECT INVESTIGATION OF PRIVATE PROPERTY

A large portion of Louis Henkin's work, *Arms Control and Inspection in American Law*,[77] is concerned with the legal and constitutional problems of investigation of private activities. Such problems would be of much less significance for inspectors in the Soviet Union, since in accordance with the provisions of the Constitution mentioned above, nearly all means of production are owned by the state and controlled by state agencies. Private ownership is strictly limited to the categories specified in Articles 7, 9, and 10 of the Constitution; thus under Article 7, a collective farm household has rights of use of a small plot of land attached to the house and rights of ownership in the house, livestock, poultry and minor agricultural implements; also under Article 9, individual peasants and handicraftsmen are permitted to have small private enterprises, provided that they do not use hired labor; finally, under Article 10, all citizens are empowered to own income and savings derived from work, a dwelling house, a supplemental husbandry, and articles of household and personal use. The Soviet armaments industry is completely in the hands of the state.[78] Private ownership of firearms is subject to strict regulation. Illegal possession or manufacture of firearms may be punished by confinement in a correctional labor colony for as long as two years under Article 218 of the Russian Criminal Code. Thus the inspectors would encounter relatively few problems arising from the property rights of individual Soviet citizens.

Problems relating to the power of the inspectors to search the person and the premises of private Soviet citizens could loom somewhat larger.

---

77. *Supra* note 1.
78. "The following private trades and the issuance of licenses for them are prohibited: . . . the manufacture and repair of cutting weapons and firearms, the manufacture of explosive and flammable substances, including pyrotechnical items—fireworks, Bengal fires, etc." Rules of Registration of Private Craftsmen, *supra* note 54.

Authorizing legislation might be needed, although the Soviet Constitution would not have to be changed. Whether or not violation of the disarmament agreement were made a crime, the inspectorate would need powers similar to those of Soviet police agencies, if it were to detain, search, and interrogate private citizens in order to obtain evidence of treaty violations. It is necessary therefore to examine the provisions of the Soviet Constitution and of Soviet criminal procedure law governing criminal investigation. The following discussion is based upon the Code of Criminal Procedure of the Russian Republic,[79] but there are no important differences in the codes of the other republics.

Pre-trial procedure in criminal cases begins with an "inquiry," which may include such measures as search, seizure, examination, detention and interrogation of suspects, interrogation of victims and witnesses. This inquiry may be conducted by any one of several authorized "agencies of inquiry," such as agencies of the police, agencies of state security, or agencies of state fire supervision. In cases of minor crimes, the agency of inquiry prepares a record which forms the basis for trial; in cases of major crimes, the case is turned over by the procuracy to an "investigator," who conducts a more formal "preliminary investigation" of the crime, preparatory to the issuance of an indictment and the commencement of a trial.

The agency of inquiry may summon or, if sufficient grounds exist, detain a person suspected of committing a crime. No sanction of a court or procurator is required for the initial apprehension of a suspect or for his detention for the first 24 hours by an agency of inquiry; within 24 hours, the procuracy must be notified of the detention, and within the next 48 hours, it must decide either to make an accusation and present it to the accused person or to order the suspect to be released. In exceptional cases, the procurator may order confinement up to ten days without presenting the accusation to the accused person.

Article 127 of the Soviet Constitution and Article 11 of the RSFSR Code of Criminal Procedure provide that "No person may be placed under arrest except by a decree of a court or with the sanction of a procurator."

---

79. *Ugolovno-protsessual'nyi kodeks RSFSR: ofitsial'nyi tekst s izmeneniiami na 1 ianvaria 1962 g. i s philozheniiami postateino-sistematizirovannykh materialov {Criminal Procedure Code of the RSFSR: Official Text with Amendments as of January 1, 1962, and with Appendix of Materials Systematized by Articles}* (Moscow, 1962). Article 89. The Code, as amended to July 3, 1965, is translated and discussed in Berman and Spindler *supra* note 5. The standard but unofficial Soviet commentary is V. A. Boldyrev, general editor, *Nauchno-prakticheskii kommentarii k ugolovno-protsessual'nomu kodeksu RSFSR {A Scholarly and Practical Commentary to the Criminal Procedure Code of the RSFSR}* (Moscow, 1963). Relevant articles of the Code are printed in the Documentation, *infra* p. 69.

The Russian legal term *arest,* which is usually translated, as it is here, by the English term "arrest," has in fact a somewhat different meaning. In Anglo-American criminal procedure, "arrest" refers to the initial apprehension of a suspected criminal; in Soviet procedure, *arest* as used in Article 127 of the Constitution refers to the binding of an accused person over for further investigation, which, as was mentioned immediately above, may occur up to 72 (24 plus 48) hours after the initial detention. In accordance with Article 172 of the Code of Criminal Procedure, the agency of inquiry may conduct a personal search of the suspect under detention.

Agencies of inquiry also have broad powers to search and seize private property. Article 128 of the Constitution of the USSR provides that "the inviolability of the homes of citizens and the privacy of correspondence are protected by law." Despite this broad language, Soviet legislation has given agencies of inquiry and preliminary investigation considerably broader powers of search and seizure than are permissible in the United States and it has never been suggested by any Soviet commentator that the constitutionality of this legislation was doubtful. (Even if it were unconstitutional, such legislation — being based on all-union law — would not be subject to judicial annulment.)[80] These powers are enumerated in detail in the RSFSR Code of Criminal Procedure, Articles 167-177, reproduced below in the Documentation, and in the charters of various Soviet investigative and inspection agencies.[81] Sanction of a court is never necessary for a search, and the sanction of a procurator is not necessary "in instances not permitting delay," or "in the event that it is necessary to remove certain articles or documents of significance for a case, and if it is known precisely where they are and who has them." Whether or not permission of the procuracy is required for search and seizure, there is a requirement that there be "sufficient grounds" for the search, a requirement analogous to the American requirement of probable cause. If this requirement were strictly interpreted, it might hinder the inspectorate in making systematic inspections of premises where it had no reason to expect to find any evidence of violation. Articles and documents discovered in the course of a search having "a relation to the case" or "prohibited from circulation" may be seized. Seizure of postal and telegraphic correspondence requires approval or a procurator or a court. Most documents which would evidence violation of a disarmament agreement would contain military information constituting a state secret, and thus problems

80. See *supra* p. 5.
81. *Supra* note 71.

39

might arise in connection with the second paragraph of Article 67 of the Code of Criminal Procedure, which requires that seizure of documents containing information which constitutes a state secret shall be conducted only with the sanction of a procurator and in accordance with a procedure agreed upon with the director of the respective institution.

Presumably the inspectors would not be concerned with *arest* in the technical Soviet sense, but with detention, search and seizure; presumably, their inspection functions would be analogous to those of Soviet "agencies of inquiry," including the regular police (*militsiia*) and the state security agencies, rather than to those of the agencies of preliminary investigation. Nevertheless, they might require the power to detain a person for more than 24-72 hours without the necessity that an accusation be brought against him. In any event, a verification agreement should contain a clear definition of the investigatory powers of the inspectorate. In particular, it should be made clear whether or not it would have all the powers of a Soviet agency of inquiry, and whether it would need additional powers to deal with correspondence, secret documents, and searches where there were not "sufficient grounds" for suspicion.

It should be noted that a suspect, prior to accusation, has no right to counsel, and that an accused person also has no right to counsel until the presentation to him of the investigator's draft of the indictment prior to trial or, where there is not a preliminary investigation, at the moment he is brought to trial; except that minors and mental or physical defectives are entitled to counsel from the moment the accusation is presented to them.

D. INTERROGATION OF PRIVATE SOVIET CITIZENS

Interrogation of private citizens involves many problems in addition to those discussed above in connection with the interrogation of Soviet officals. Soviet law contains no provision requiring suspects or accused persons to testify, and expressly forbids an investigator or person conducting an inquiry to solicit testimony by force, threats, or any other illegal measure (RSFSR Code of Criminal Procedure, Article 20). Indeed, a suspect or accused person may refuse to answer any question, whether or not his answer would tend to be self-incriminating. However, adverse inferences may be drawn from a refusal to answer. Witnesses, on the other hand, as distinct from suspects and accused persons, may be punished for refusing to testify, although the maximum penalty ("correctional tasks," which in practice means a withholding of up to 25 per cent of monthly wages, up to six months) is relatively light (RSFSR Criminal Code, Article 182); moreover, no Soviet court or agency has a power comparable to that of American courts to incarcerate an uncooperative witness, or impose prohibitive fines upon him, for civil contempt, and so compel him to choose between testifying and remaining in jail or paying large sums of money indefinitely. Thus in order to give inspectors under disarmament agreement sufficient powers to overcome the silence of persons being questioned, new Soviet legislation might be required to increase, for these purposes, the sanctions now available against recalcitrant witnesses.

Soviet law also imposes no sanction upon a suspect or accused who answers falsely. Witnesses, however, as distinct from suspects or accused, are punishable by deprivation of freedom up to one year or by correctional tasks for knowingly giving false testimony in court or in the course of a preliminary investigation of inquiry (Article 181). Again, the existing sanction may be inadequate for the purpose of inspection under a disarmament agreement. For one thing, a prosecution for perjury requires time, proof, and the cooperation of Soviet law enforcement and judicial officers, and the contingent nature of these factors might reduce its deterrent power. In addition, the inspectors would be less interestd in a prosecution than in a determination of whether or not the person being interrogated was or was not telling the truth. For these purposes, they might want to use such devices as lie detectors or "truth serum." No Soviet legal provisions dealing with lie detectors or truth serum, and, indeed, no reports of their use in the Soviet Union, have come to the attention of the authors. Moreover, Soviet jurists have denounced their use in the United States.[82] If in fact Soviet investigators do not use such methods because they consider them unreliable, the Soviet government might be reluctant to give legal recognition to results obtained with their aid, or even to allow their use.

E. GRANTING IMMUNITY TO INFORMERS

There would be serious legal and practical obstacles to giving the inspection organization the power to grant immunity to informers. A major problem is created by the existence of two separate systems of sanctions in the Soviet Union, those administered by the State and those administered by the Communist Party.

---

82. American use of "truth serum" and lie detectors was severely criticised in a Soviet article published late in 1964. V. M. Nikolaichik, " 'Syvorotka pravdy' i 'lai-detektor'—vozvrashchenie k inkvizitsionnomu protsessu" ["Truth Serum" and the "Lie Detector"—A Return to the Methods of the Inquisition], *Sovetskoe gosudarstvo i pravo {Soviet State and Law}*, 1964, no. 12, p. 120.

The promise of immunity from state sanctions might be viewed with some skepticism by Soviet citizens for a variety of reasons. One reason would be the absence of a constitutional provision against *ex post facto* laws, a fact which has been forcefully emphasized by at least one recent instance of retroactive imposition of the death penalty for certain crimes.[83] Secondly, the value of immunity from prosecution for specific crimes would be slight in view of the fact that most Soviet citizens depend upon the good will of Soviet government agencies for their jobs, their housing, and many other aspects of their lives; thus there are available a variety of methods of indirect retaliation which are technically compatible with a formal immunity. Finally, a relatively high degree of political insecurity based on the existence of terror in the past and the continuing fear of a possible return to terror in the future would greatly reduce the value of a promise of immunity.

With respect to Party sanctions it should be kept in mind that many if not most of the officials with whom the inspectors would deal would be members of the Communist Party of the Soviet Union.[84] The Party Rules places a solemn obligation upon every Party member to obey higher Party authorities and to keep Party secrets.[85] The imposition of Party sanctions, which range from reprimand to expulsion,[86] can have an adverse effect upon one's career in the USSR as severe as dishonorable discharge from the armed services might have in the United States. Neither the Party Rules nor Party practice contain any restrictions upon punishment for actions that were not offenses at the time they were created. It seems unlikely, therefore, that any promise of immunity against state sanctions could be effective against an order of silence transmitted through Party channels.

The only effective means for granting immunity might be to permit the informer and his family to leave the USSR permanently. However, the possibility of Soviet acceptance of this alternative must be seen in the light of the Soviet policy against emigration. Soviet law expressly prohibits departure from the USSR without specific permission from the Ministry of Foreign Affairs. In practice such permission has been very difficult to obtain for persons who wish to emigrate or for whole families which wish to leave the USSR at the same time. Leaving without permission is punishable under Article 1 of the Law on Criminal Responsibility for Crimes

83. Berman, *supra* note 5, at pp. 86 and 403.
84. Nicholas De Witt, *Education and Professional Employment in the USSR* (Washington, 1961), pp. 533-537; United States Senate, Committee on Government Operations, *Staffing Procedures and Problems in the Soviet Union* (Washington, 1963).
85. Article 2, printed in the Documentation, *infra* p. 59.
86. Articles 9-12 of the Party Rules, printed in the Documentation, *infra* p. 60.

Against the State,[87] which classifies "fleeing abroad or refusing to return from abroad" as high treason for which the death penalty may be applied.

F. COMPENSATION FOR DAMAGE TO SOVIET GOVERNMENT PROPERTY AND TO SOVIET CITIZENS

In the course of their operations the inspectors would probably cause damage to the property of the Soviet government and to the property and persons of private Soviet citizens. In some instances it might be necessary to destroy property in order to carry out effective inspection. If the inspectorate were to control its own means of transportation, it is probable that some accidents would occur involving personal injury to Soviet citizens and property loss for Soviet citizens or Soviet state organizations.

Unless the inspectors were granted immunity, they would be liable for the damage they caused under the provisions of both Soviet criminal and civil law. Soviet criminal law makes punishable the intentional and in some instances the negligent destruction or damaging of property, with penalties ranging from a fine not exceeding one hundred rubles to a maximum of ten years' deprivation of freedom, depending upon the seriousness of the offense (RSFSR Criminal Code, Articles 98, 99, 149, 150).

Both the individual inspectors and the inspectorate would be civilly liable (absent immunity) for harm caused negligently and in some instances for harm caused innocently (without negligence) in the course of inspection operations.[88] Article 88 of the Fundamental Principles of Civil Legislation provides that one who causes harm must compensate for it unless he proves the harm was caused without his fault. This Article also makes organizations liable for harm caused by employees in performance of their duties. Article 90 provides that organizations and citizens whose activity is connected with increased danger for those nearby (transport organizations, industrial enterprises, builders, owners of automobiles, *etc.*), must compensate for harm caused by the source of increased danger, unless they show that the harm arose as a result of an insuperable force or the intent of the victim.

Assuming that the inspection agency was authorized by law or treaty to destroy property where necessary to carry out its objectives, it apparently would not be liable for such destruction, in view of the last clause of

---

87. Identical with Article 64 of the Criminal Code of the RSFSR, printed in the Documentation, *infra* p. 89.
88. See generally Whitmore Gray, "Soviet Tort Law: The New Principles Annotated," *University of Illinois Law Forum,* Vol. 1964, no. 1, p. 180. Also see Civil Code of the RSFSR, *supra* note 18, Articles 444-471; and see *infra* p. 107.

Article 88. To avoid popular resentment, it might be wise for the inspectorate to submit to a liability similar to that imposed upon Soviet government agencies, which are required by law to pay compensation for private property taken for public use.[89] Both the individual inspectors and the inspectorate (under the doctrine of *respondeat superior* stated in Article 88) would be liable for damage negligently caused to property. Under Article 90, both the inspectors and the inspectorate would be liable for damage caused by their motor vehicle, airplane and other "sources of increased danger." Such liability would be imposed even where the inspectors were not at fault.

It would be important to provide a method whereby the Soviet government and citizens injured by the inspection organization or by one of the inspectors could have a fair and speedy remedy for the harm done. One possibility would be for the inspection agency itself to submit to the jurisdiction of the Soviet courts for the determination of liability and the measure of damages, while retaining its immunity from execution of the resulting judgment as a protection against any excesses by the Soviet courts.[90] An alternative would be to have liability assumed by an agency of the Soviet government, perhaps the Foreign Insurance Administration of the USSR,[91] in return for a cash premium plus reimbursement for damage caused intentionally in the exercise of inspection privileges, or perhaps in return for assumption by the United States Government of liability for damages caused by inspectors in the United States. The Soviet Union might be quite willing to submit to such a reciprocal arrangement because the judgments returned by Soviet courts in property damage and personal injury cases are generally much smaller than those in similar cases in United States courts. There is no recovery for mental suffering or for medical care (insofar as the latter is administered by the state without charge),[92] and property destroyed or seized for public use is valued at official rates which do not exceed and often are lower than the market price.[93]

---

89. Property-taking procedures and compensation are governed by Svodnyi zakon o rekvizitsii i konfiskatsii [Codified Law on Requisition and Confiscation], *SU RSFSR,* 1927 no. 38, item 248. The application of this law and amendments thereto subsequent to 1927 are discussed in I. L. Braude, *Vozmeshchenie ushcherba pri iz"iatii zemli {Compensation for Loss in Land Taking}* (Moscow, 1960).

90. Such a procedure would be similar to that under the United States Tort Claims Act, 28 USC §2671-80 (1964).

91. The standard liability insurance policies of this agency in most respects follow customary international practice. They contain exceptions freeing the insurer from liability for damage caused by the intent or gross negligence of the insured. Pravila strakhovaniia grazhdanskoi otvetvennosti [Rules for Insuring Civil Liability], approved by an order of The Ministry of Finances of the USSR of December 2, 1959, no. 336, printed in *Sbornik, supra* note 43, p. 238.

92. Gray, *supra* note 88, at pp. 187-189.

93. Braude, *supra* note 89, at pp. 28-44.

44

CONCLUSIONS

Our study has been primarily concerned with two questions: (1) How could the effectiveness and the safety of an international inspectorate be secured under Soviet law? and (2) What limits woud have to be placed upon the powers of an international inspectorate in order to protect the legal rights and interests of Soviet citizens and of the Soviet state? Although we have by no means found complete answers to these questions, we believe that several important conclusions can be drawn from the materials that we have presented (including the legislative and other documentation that follows our analysis).

The first of these conclusions is that on the Soviet side (as on the American) there are, indeed, legal obstacles, and not only political obstacles, to any system of on-site or aerial inspection of disarmament. It is not true, in other words, that all that is needed in order to maintain a system of inspection on or over Soviet territory is for the Soviet leaders to be persuaded that it is in their interests to permit it. Assuming that they firmly desired to cooperate in maintaining such a system of international inspection, conflicts must nevertheless be anticipated between the inspectorate, on the one hand, and Soviet citizens and governmental organizations, on the other, which would require resolution under settled rules and procedures conforming to Soviet standards of justice. We have seen that if international inspectors in Soviet territory damaged property or caused personal injuries, legal interests of Soviet citizens would be affected and legal claims could be presented. More important, if international inspectors wished to seize property, search the premises and persons of Soviet citizens, interrogate them, seize documents and correspondence, or even simply bring their own equipment into the Soviet Union, they would have to make use not only of the good will of the Soviet government but also of the techniques and the concepts of Soviet law. Even if conflicts over such matters never actually materialized, it would be necessary to agree in advance as to how they would be resolved if they did materialize. Indeed, such advance agreement would be an important means of preventing them from materializing.

Hypothetically, to be sure, one might insist that all Soviet legal claims against an international inspectorate be barred, and that it be exempted

45

from all Soviet legal requirements. Such a solution, however, would not only be unacceptable to the Soviet Union (just as a counter-proposal to such effect would be unacceptable to the United States); it would also be a denial of the very possibility of creating the kind of international legal order that an agreement for disarmament presupposes. The whole idea of such an agreement is for nations to subject themselves, in one major aspect of their activities affecting world peace, to the binding force of mutually accepted rules and procedures. To erect the inspectorate into a superstate unlimited by the rights of persons and of nations would only be to create a new form of despotism. One might, to be sure, remove questions of *enforcement* of inspection from a national to an international or supranational level, so that any claims by Soviet citizens would be settled by international or supranational procedures and any demands of the inspectorate within the Soviet Union would be implemented by an international or supranational police force or army; even this, however, would by no means eliminate the operation of Soviet law, but would in fact make it all the more necessary to secure agreement in advance concerning what rules of Soviet law would be applicable by the enforcement authority in the event of infringement by the inspectorate of the legitimate interests of Soviet citizens and of the Soviet state.

Our second conclusion is that while, as we have just indicated, Soviet law (like American law) presents obstacles to the negotiation and enforcement of a disarmament agreement calling for international inspection, it also presents a generally suitable framework for overcoming a great many of those obstacles. Soviet law, in other words, is sufficiently mature, sufficiently stable, and at the same time sufficiently flexible, to permit a satisfactory resolution of a great many types of conflict that might arise between the international inspectorate, on the one hand, and Soviet citizens and state organizations on the other.

We have seen that the USSR has a highly developed legal system which provides reasonable standards and workable procedures for the adjudication of criminal and civil cases and for the supervision of administrative acts. No major changes in the general structure of Soviet law would be required to accommodate civil claims for harm done either by or to an international inspectorate, in order to permit it to conduct necessary interrogation, search and seizure, and the like. In addition, Soviet foreign relations law provides many examples of the kinds of special accommodation that international inspectors might require; thus Soviet consular and diplomatic law, the Convention on the Privileges and Immunities of the United Nations, and, in particular, the Convention on the Legal Capacity, Privileges, and Immunities of Members of the Council for Mutual Economic Assistance—all contain provisions upon which an agreement for verification of arms control or disarmament might build.

At the same time, while the general structure of the Soviet legal system could be left without substantial change, a very large number of particular changes would have to be made in Soviet law before an international spectorate could operate effectively on Soviet soil. Inspection of disarmament—at least, under most plans that have been proposed on the American side—would involve a substantially greater intrusion into the affairs of the Soviet government and into the private lives of Soviet citizens than any foreign presence on Soviet soil has hitherto required. At present, for example, foreign diplomats can be expelled for photographing military installations; presumably international inspectors could not be. A foreign businessman cannot examine the records of a Soviet state trading agency or state enterprise with which he is dealing; an inspector might need the right to do so. (On the other hand, inspectors would presumably have no need to see, much less to publish, archives of intra-Kremlin politics or private intra-family correspondence.) Our study has shown that the Soviet legal system is sufficiently flexible to permit such particular changes to be made with relative ease. There are no insurmountable Constitutional problems involved, as there might be in the United States; for example, the granting to the inspectorate of powers of search and seizure without a warrant, while it would require detailed implementing legislation giving the inspectorate certain procuratorial powers, would probably not require any Constitutional amendments. And there are no serious political problems in securing new legislation, or even new Constitutional amendments, once the Communist Party leadership is convinced of the desirability thereof.

We would add as a separate, third conclusion the fact that changes in Soviet legislation introduced to safeguard the work of an international inspectorate, and to define the limits of its powers, could also help to create political pressures for continued obedience to an inspection arrangement. We have seen that the political, social, and moral education of Soviet citizens is considered to be one of the major tasks of Soviet law. Accordingly, legal principles related to inspection of disarmament could be incorporated into Soviet law in such a way as to help to educate Soviet officials as well as other Soviet citizens in the goals and ideals of disarmament. Appropriate changes in the Communist Party Rules as well as in the Constitution, the Statute on the Procuracy, the criminal and civil codes,

47

and many other Soviet legal sources, could have, over the years, an important psychological effect in enhancing the value of disarmament and of inspection, in the eyes of the Soviet people. This in turn could present serious political obstacles if the Soviet leadership ever wished to perpetrate secret violations of a disarmament agreement.

Our fourth conclusion is less optimistic. There are certain areas of Soviet political and economic life into which an international inspectorate could not penetrate, regardless of any changes that might be made in the Soviet legal system; yet such penetration might be necessary, under most types of inspection, in order to guarantee the active cooperation of Soviet officials in carrying out inspection functions.

We say most types of inspection, rather than all types, because there is at least one—aerial inspection by planes or satellites based outside the USSR—which would not require active cooperation by Soviet officials and which therefore would present no insuperable obstacles to legal regulation (assuming that the Soviet Union agreed to permit it). Such aerial inspection would, indeed, require many changes in present Soviet law in order to provide immunity from espionage laws, coordination with Soviet air traffic control systems, liability for airplane crashes, and the like, but all this could be done without dependence upon Soviet sources of supply of goods, services, and information, and hence without intrusion into hidden areas of Soviet political and economic life.

Most types of inspection, however, would require—as we have seen—the active day-to-day cooperation of Soviet officials, who would be needed to provide facilities, offer protection, assure possibilities of investigation, answer questions, and the like. If however, Soviet officials, acting under secret instructions, withheld their cooperation and instead conspired to frustrate and mislead the inspectorate, its work would be seriously impeded; more than that, it might have no way of ascertaining that it was being deceived. Thus even if Soviet law were changed so as to give international inspectors etxraordinary powers, enabling them to go where they wanted, see what they wanted, ask what they wanted, take what they wanted, do what they wanted, nevertheless they might come up against a wall of secrecy and deception that would block all their powers.

What has been said of the possibility of deception by Soviet officials would also be true in other countries in which an international inspectorate might operate, including the United States. In any country it is conceivable that the executive authority, impelled especially by the military and counterintelligence departments, would issue secret orders to subordinate officials, in violation of the disarmament agreement and of the national laws enacted in accordance therewith, for the purpose of "cheating."

The problem of detecting any such cheating—and, at least equally important, the problem of proving that such cheating has not taken place if in fact it has not—is especially acute in a country like the Soviet Union, in which responsible officials are generally members of the Communist Party and hence subject to strict Party discipline requiring obedience to secret orders from Party superiors. Moreover, not only the munitions industry is operated by such officials, but virtually the entire national economy, including science and technology. That the Party can keep important secrets has been demonstrated many times in Soviet history. Even a Soviet law requiring all persons, including Party members, to answer truthfully all questions put by the international inspectorate would not prevail against secret Party instructions, or, indeed, a secret statute, nullifying such a law. Nor can we think of any way for an inspectorate to grant effective immunity against the expulsion of a Party member—with its consequent disgrace and its threat to the member's entire career—for breach of Party discipline.

It may be thought by some that our fourth conclusion vitiates our second and third conclusions. We would disagree. It must be remembered that we are starting from the hypothesis of a disarmament agreement. Presumably neither the United States nor the Soviet Union would enter into such an agreement until each is convinced that the other side really wants it and really means to abide by it. If the agreement, and enforcement of the agreement, are not in the interests of both sides, presumably there will be no agreement and no system of enforcement. The problem is a narrower one than that of attempting to maintain—by retaliatory measures or otherwise—a disarmament agreement against the will of a state that is party to it. What our fourth conclusion demonstrates is that even if both sides wanted to maintain disarmament with effective international inspection, no system that they could establish to achieve these goals would give 100 per cent assurance of compliance. A certain amount of trust, and of willingness to take risks, would therefore be required to support the continuing successful operation of any inspection agreement with the Soviet Union, just as such a trust and such a willingness are required to support any other kind of genuine agreement between two parties. Confidence in inspection must undoubtedly be based partly on the mutual interest of both sides in maintaining disarmament. Our second and third conclusions point to ways in which Soviet law could be used to lessen the risks that inspection involves and hence to bolster confidence in it still further. The fact that cheating is possible—on both sides—and that such cheating on the Soviet side would be aided by the existence of a Party discipline in the Soviet Union that stands outside and above the Soviet legal system, do, indeed, impose a strain on that confidence, but do not necessarily destroy it.

We return, finally, to our underlying concern, which is the role of law as a channel for, and an obstacle to, cooperation between nations—and especially between nations that wish to cooperate but are uncertain as to how cooperation can be achieved. We have seen that any discussion of inspection under a disarmament agreement must include an analysis of the ways in which law can be used as a vehicle of inspection. Such an analysis, we believe, brings an element of realism into the discussion, and into any international disarmament negotiations, that is otherwise lacking. Moreover, we would repeat what we have stressed in our introduction: that even if disarmament is not possible, and even if it is not desirable, analysis of the changes in national law that it would require helps to clarify other serious problems of international relations—problems of trade, cultural exchange, scientific cooperation, tourism, diplomacy, and the like—whose solutions may be closer at hand.

DOCUMENTATION

I. CONSTITUTION (BASIC LAW) OF THE UNION OF SOVIET SOCIALIST REPUBLICS (Excerpts)

CHAPTER I

The Social Structure

Article 1

The Union of Soviet Socialist Republics is a socialist state of workers and peasants.

Articles 2-3 [text omitted]

Article 4

The socialist system of economy and socialist ownership of the instruments and means of production, which were established as a result of the liquidation of the capitalist system of economy, the abolition of private ownership of the instruments and means of production, and the annihilation of exploitation of man by man, comprise the economic foundation of the USSR.

Article 5

Socialist ownership in the USSR exists either in the form of state ownership (belonging to the whole people) or in the form of cooperative and collective-farm ownership (ownership of individual collective farms, ownership of cooperative societies).

Article 6

The land, its mineral wealth, waters, forests, plants, factories, underground and open-pit mines, rail, water, and air transport, banks, communications, large state-organized agricultural enterprises (state farms, machine-tractor stations, *etc.*), as well as municipal enterprises and the basic housing fund in the cities and industrial localities, are state ownership, that is, belong to the whole people.

Article 7

The social enterprises of collective farms and cooperative organizations, with their livestock and implements, the products produced by the collective farms and cooperative organizations, as well as their social buildings, constitute the social, socialist ownership of collective farms and cooperative organizations.

Every collective farm household, in addition to its basic income from the social collective farm economy, shall have for its personal use a small plot of household land, and, as its personal ownership, a subsidiary husbandry on the plot, a dwelling house, livestock, poultry and minor agricultural implements—in accordance with the charter of the agricultural artel.

Article 8

The land occupied by collective farms shall be secured to them for their use free of charge and for an unlimited time, that is, in perpetuity.

Article 9

Alongside the socialist system of economy, which is the predominant form of economy in the USSR, the small private economy of individual peasants and handicraftsmen based on personal labor and precluding the exploitation of the labor of others, shall be permitted by law.

Article 10

The right of personal ownership of citizens in their incomes and savings from work, in their dwelling-houses and subsidiary husbandries, in articles of domestic economy and household use, and articles of personal consumption and convenience, as well as the right of citizens to inherit personal property, shall be protected by law.

Article 11

The economic life of the USSR shall be determined and directed by the state national economic plan, in the interests of increasing the social wealth, of steadily raising the material and cultural level of the working people, of consolidating the independence of the USSR, and of strengthening its defensive capacity.

Article 12 [text omitted]

CHAPTER II

The State Structure

Article 13

The Union of Soviet Socialist Republics is a federal state, formed on the basis of a voluntary union of equal Soviet Socialist Republics, namely:

The Russian Soviet Federated Socialist Republic
The Ukrainian Soviet Socialist Republic
The Byelorussian Soviet Socialist Republic
The Uzbek Soviet Socialist Republic
The Kazakh Soviet Socialist Republic
The Georgian Soviet Socialist Republic
The Azerbaidzhan Soviet Socialist Republic
The Lithuanian Soviet Socialist Republic
The Moldavian Soviet Socialist Republic
The Latvian Soviet Socialist Republic
The Kirgiz Soviet Socialist Republic
The Tadzhik Soviet Socialist Republic
The Armenian Soviet Socialist Republic
The Turkmen Soviet Socialist Republic
The Estonian Soviet Socialist Republic

Article 14

The following shall be subject to the jurisdiction of the Union of Soviet Socialist Republics, as represented by its higher agencies of state power and agencies of state administration:

(a) Representation of the USSR in international relations, conclusion, ratification and denunciation of treaties of the USSR with other states, establishment of a general procedure concerning the relations of union republics with foreign states;

(b) Questions of war and peace;

(c) Admission of new republics into the USSR;

(d) Control over the observance of the Constitution of the USSR, and ensuring conformity of the constitutions of the union republics with the Constitution of the USSR;

(e) Confirmation of alterations of boundaries between union republics;

(f) Confirmation of the formation of new autonomous Republics and autonomous regions within union republics;

(g) Organization of the defense of the USSR, direction of all the Armed Forces of the USSR, establishment of fundamental principles governing the organization of the military formations of the union republics;

(h) Foreign trade on the basis of state monopoly;

(i) Safeguarding the security of the state;

(j) Establishment of the national economic plans of the USSR;

(k) Confirmation of the unified state budget of the USSR and of the report on its fulfillment; establishment of taxes and revenues which enter into the formation of the union, the republican, and the local budgtes;

(l) Administration of the banks, industrial and agricultural institutions and enterprises, as well as of trade enterprises of all-union subordination; general direction of industry and construction of union-republican subordination;

(m) Administration of transport and communications of all-union significance;

(n) Direction of the monetary and credit system;

(o) Organization of state insurance;

(p) Contracting and granting of loans;

(q) Establishment of fundamental principles of land use and of the use of mineral wealth, forests, and waters;

(r) Establishment of fundamental principles in the areas of education and public health;

(s) Organization of a uniform system of national economic accounting;

(t) Establishment of fundamental principles of labor legislation;

(u) Establishment of fundamental principles of legislation on court organization and the court procedure; fundamental principles of civil and criminal legislation;

(v) Legislation concerning union citizenship; legislation concerning rights of foreigners;

(w) Establishment of fundamental principles of legislation concerning marriage and the family;

(x) Issuance of all-union acts of amnesty.

Articles 15-18 [text omitted]

Article 18-a

Each union republic shall have the right to enter into direct relations with foreign states and to conclude agreements and exchange diplomatic and consular representatives with them.

Article 18-b

Each union republic shall have its own republican military formations.

Article 19 [text omitted]

Article 20

In the event of divergence between a law of a union republic and an all-union law, the all-union law shall prevail.

Articles 21-29 [text omitted]

CHAPTER III

The Higher Agencies of State Power in the Union of Soviet Socialist Republics

Article 30

The highest agency of state power in the USSR shall be the Supreme Soviet of the USSR.

Article 31 [text omitted]

Article 32

The legislative power of the USSR shall be exercised exclusively by the Supreme Sovit of the USSR.

Articles 33-48 [text omitted]

Article 49

The Presidium of the Supreme Soviet of the USSR shall:

(a) Convene the sessions of the Supreme Soviet of the USSR;
(b) Issue edicts;
(c) Give interpretations of the laws in force of the USSR;
(d) Dissolve the Supreme Soviet of the USSR in conformity with Article 47 of the Constitution of the USSR and call new elections;
(e) Conduct nation-wide polls (referendums) on its own initiative or on the request of one of the union republics;
(f) Annul decrees and orders of the Council of Ministers of the USSR and of the Councils of Ministers of the union republics if they do not conform to law;
(g) In the interval between sessions of the Supreme Soviet of the USSR,
(h) Institute orders and medals of the USSR and establish honorary titles of the USSR;
(i) Award orders and medals and confer honorary titles of the USSR;
(j) Exercise the right of pardon;
(k) Establish military titles, diplomatic ranks and other special titles;
(l) Appoint and remove the high command of the Armed Forces of the USSR;
(m) In the interval between sessions of the Supreme Soviet of the USSR, declare a state of war in the event of military attack on the USSR, or when necessary for the fulfillment of international treaty obligations concerning mutual defense against aggression;
(n) Declare general or partial mobilization;
(o) Ratify and denounce international treaties of the USSR;
(p) Appoint and recall plenipotentiary representatives of the USSR to foreign states;

(q) Receive the letters of credence and recall of diplomatic representatives accredited to it by foreign states;

(r) Proclaim martial law in separate localities or throughout the USSR in the interests of the defense of the USSR or of the maintenance of social order and state security.

Articles 50-56 [text omitted]

CHAPTER IV

The Higher Agencies of State Power
In the Union Republics
[text omitted]

CHAPTER V

The Agencies of State Administration of the
Union of Soviet Socialist Republics

Article 64

The highest executive and administrative agency of state power of the Union of Soviet Socialist Republics shall be the Council of Ministers of the USSR.

Article 65 [text omitted]

Article 66

The Council of Ministers of the USSR shall issue decrees and orders on the basis and in pursuance of the laws in force, and shall verify their execution.

Article 67

Decrees and orders of the Council of Ministers of the USSR shall be binding throughout the territory of the USSR.

Article 68

The Council of Ministers of the USSR shall:

(a) Coordinate and direct the work of the Supreme Council of National Economy of the USSR of the Council of Ministers of the USSR, of all-union and union-republican ministries of the USSR, of state committees of councils of ministers of the USSR, and of other institutions under its jurisdiction;

(b) Adopt measures for the realization of the national economic plan and the state budget, and for the strengthening of the credit and monetary system;

(c) Adopt measures for the maintenance of social order, for the defense of the interests of the state, and for the protection of the rights of citizens;

(d) Exercise general direction in the sphere of relations with foreign states;

(e) Determine the annual contingent of citizens subject to being called up for active military service and direct the general organization of the Armed Forces of the country;

(f) Form state committees of the USSR, and also whenever necessary, special committees and chief administrations under the Council of Ministers of the USSR for matters of economic, cultural, and defense organization.

Article 69

The Council of Ministers of the USSR shall have the right, with respect to those branches of administration and economy that come within the jurisdiction of the USSR, to suspend decrees and orders of the councils of ministers of the union republics and to annul orders and instructions of ministers of the USSR.

Articles 79-78 [text omitted]

CHAPTER VI

The Agencies of State Administration of the Union Republics
[text omitted]

CHAPTER VII

The Higher Agencies of State Power of Autonomous Soviet Socialist Republics
[text omitted]

CHAPTER VIII

The Local Agencies of State Power
[text omitted]

CHAPTER IX

The Courts and the Procurary

Article 102

In the USSR justice shall be administered by the Supreme Court of the USSR, the supreme courts of the union republics, the courts of territories, regions, autonomous republics, autonomous regions and areas, the special courts of the USSR established by decree of the Supreme Soviet of the USSR, and the people's courts.

Article 103 [text omitted]

Article 104

The Supreme Court of the USSR shall be the highest judicial agency. The Supreme Court of the USSR shall be vested with the supervision of the judicial activities of all the judicial agencies of the USSR and of the union republics.

Article 105-109 [text omitted]

Article 110

Judicial proceedings shall be conducted in the language of the union republic, autonomous republic or autonomous region, persons not knowing this language being secured the opportunity of fully acquainting themselves with the material of the case through an interpreter and likewise the right to use their native language in court.

Article 111

Examination of cases in all courts of the USSR shall be open, insofar as exceptions are not provided for by law, with the accused being secured the right to defense.

Article 112

Judges shall be independent and subordinate only to the law.

Article 113

Supreme supervision of strict observance of the law by all ministries and institutions subordinate to them, as well as by individual officials and citizens of the USSR, shall be vested in the Procurator-General of the USSR.

Article 114-116 [text omitted]

Article 117

The agencies of the procuracy shall exercise their functions independently of any local agencies whatsoever, being subordinate solely to the Procurator-General of the USSR.

CHAPTER X

Fundamental Rights and Duties of Citizens

Articles 118-125 [text omitted]

Article 126

In conformity with the interests of the working people, and for the purposes of developing the organizational initiative and political activity of the masses of the people, citizens of the USSR shall be assured the right to unite in social organizations: trade unions, cooperative unions, youth organizations, sport and defense organizations, cultural, technical, and scientific societies; and the most active and politically conscious citizens in the ranks of the working class, working peasants and working intelligentsia shall voluntarily unite in the Communist Party of the Soviet Union, which is the vanguard of the working people in their struggle to build communist society and is the leading core of all organizations of the working people, both social and state.

Article 127

Citizens of the USSR shall be guaranteed inviolability of the person. No person may be subjected to arrest except by decree of a court or with the sanction of a procurator.

Article 128

The inviolability of the homes of citizens and secrecy of correspondence shall be protected by law.

Article 129

The USSR shall afford the right of asylum to foreign citizens persecuted for defending the interests of the working people, or for scholarly activity, or for struggling for national liberation.

Article 130

It shall be the duty of every citizen of the USSR to observe the Constitution of the Union of Soviet Socialist Republics, to execute the laws, to maintain labor discipline, honestly to perform social duties, and to respect the rules of socialist communal life.

Article 131

It shall be the duty of every citizen of the USSR to safeguard and strengthen social, socialist property as the sacred and inviolable foundation of the Soviet system, as the source of the wealth and might of the motherland, as the source of the prosperity and culture of all the working people.

Persons committing offences against social, socialist property are enemies of the people.

Article 132

Universal military service shall be law.

Military service in the ranks of the Armed Forces of the USSR is an honorable duty of the citizens of the USSR.

Article 133

Defense of the fatherland is the sacred duty of every citizen of the USSR. Treason—violation of the oath of allegiance, desertion to the enemy, infliction of harm on the military power of the state, espionage—shall be punished with all the severity of the law as the most heinous of crimes.

CHAPTER XI

The Electoral System

Articles 134-141 [text omitted]

Article 142

It shall be the duty of every deputy to report to his electors on his work and on the work of the Soviet of Working People's Deputies, and he may be recalled at any time in the manner established by law upon decision of a majority of the electors.

CHAPTER XII

Arms, Flag, Capital

[text omitted]

CHAPTER XIII

Procedure for Amending the Constitution

Article 146

Amendment of the Constitution of the USSR shall be made only by decision of the Supreme Soviet of the USSR adopted by a majority of not less than two-thirds of the votes in each of its chambers.

II. RULES OF THE COMMUNIST PARTY OF THE SOVIET UNION.

Adopted by the Twenty-Second Congress of the Communist Party of the Soviet Union, October 31, 1961 (Excerpts)

[Preamble—text omitted]

CHAPTER I

Party Members, Their Duties And Rights

1. [text omitted]
2. A party member shall be obliged:

(a) To struggle for the creation of the material and technical base of communism; to serve as an example of the communist attitude towards labor; to raise the productivity of labor; to be a skirmisher in all that is new and progressive; to support and propagate advance methods; to master techniques, to improve his qualifications; to protect and increase social, socialist property, which is the foundation of the might and the flowering of the Soviet Motherland;

(b) Firmly and steadfastly to bring party decisions into life; to explain the policy of the party to the masses; to help strengthen and expand the party's ties with the people; to show consideration and attention to people; to respond promptly to the demands and needs of the working people;

(c) Actively to participate in the political life of the country, in the administration of state affairs, and in economic and cultural construction; to set an example in the fulfillment of his social duty; to assist in the development and strengthening of communist social relations;

(d) To master Marxist-Leninist theory, to raise his conceptual level, and to facilitate the formation and education of the man of communist society. To carry on a decisive struggle against any manifestations of bourgeois ideology, remnants of a private-property psychology, religious prejudices, and other survivals of the past; to observe the principles of communist morality, and place social interests above personal;

(e) To be an active proponent of the ideas of socialist internationalism and Soviet patriotism among the masses of the working people; to carry on a struggle against survivals of nationalism and chauvinism; to contribute by word and by deed to the strengthening of the friendship of the peoples of the USSR and the fraternal ties of the Soviet people with the peoples of the countries of the socialist camp, with the proletarians and working people of all countries;

(f) To strengthen to the utmost the conceptual and organizational unity of the party; to safeguard the party from the infiltration into its ranks of people unworthy of the lofty name of communist; to be truthful and honest before the party and the people; to display vigilance, to guard party and state secrets;

(g) To develop criticism and self-criticism, boldly to uncover shortcomings and to strive for their elimination; to struggle against ostentation, conceit, complacency, and localism; to give a decisive rebuff to all attempts at the suppression of criticism; to resist any actions causing harm to the party and to the state, and to give information of them to party agencies, up to and including the CC CPSU;

(h) To implement undeviatingly the party line with regard to the proper selection of cadres according to their political qualities and their practical abilities. To be uncompromising in all instances when Leninist principles of the selection and education of cadres are violated;

(i) To observe party and state discipline, which is equally binding on all party members. The party has one discipline, one law, for all communists, irrespective of their past services and the posts they occupy;

(j) To help to the utmost to strengthen the defensive power of the USSR; to carry on an unflagging struggle for peace and friendship among peoples;

3. A party member has the right:

(a) To elect and be elected to party agencies;

(b) To discuss freely questions of the party's policies and practical activities at party meetings, conferences and congresses, at the sessions of party committees and in party publications; to introduce proposals; openly to express and uphold his opinion prior to the adoption of a decision by the organization;

(c) To criticise any communist, irrespective of the post he holds, at party meetings, conferences and congresses, and at the plenary meetings of committees. Persons who are guilty of the suppression of criticism and of persecution for criticism must be brought to strict party responsibility, up to and including expulsion from the ranks of the party;

(d) To participate personally in party meetings and at bureau and committee sessions when the question of his activities or conduct is discussed;

(e) To address questions, declarations, and proposals to any party instance, up to and including the Central Committee of the CPSU, and to demand an answer on the substance thereof.

4-8. [text omitted]

9. A party member or candidate for membership shall be brought to responsibility for non-fulfillment of obligations laid down in the Rules and for other offenses, and the following penalties may be imposed on him: admonition, reprimand (or severe reprimand), or reprimand (or severe reprimand) with entry in the registration card. The highest measure of party punishment is expulsion from the party.

In necessary instances, a party organization may, as a party penalty, transfer a party member to candidate status for a period of up to one year. The decision of the primary party organization to transfer a party member to candidate status shall be confirmed by the district or city party committee. On the expiration of the established period, one who has been transferrd to candidate status may be readmitted in accordance with the regular procedure, with retention of his former party seniority.

For insignificant offenses, measures of party education and influence in the form of comradely criticism, party censure, warning, or reproof, must be applied.

In deciding the question of the expulsion of a member from the party, maximum attention must be shown and the grounds for the accusation preferred against a communist must be thoroughly investigated.

10. The question of expulsion of a communist from the party shall be decided by a general meeting of a primary party organization. The decision of the primary party organization on expulsion from the party shall be considered as adopted if not less than two-thirds of the party members attending the meeting have voted for it, and shall be subject to confirmation by the district or city party committee. The decision of the district or city committee to expel from the party shall take effect after confirmation by a regional or territorial committee or the Central Committee of the communist party of a union republic.

Until the confirmation by a regional or territorial committee or the Central Committee of the communist party of a union republic of the decision to expel from the CPSU, the party card or candidate card shall remain in the hands of the communist, and he shall have the right to attend closed party meetings.

An expelled party member shall retain the right of appeal, within a period of and to give information of them to party agencies, up to and including the Central Committee of the CPSU;

11. The question of bringing members or candidate members of the Central Committee of the communist party of a union republic, or of a territorial, regional, area, city or district party committee, as well as members of inspection commissions, to party responsibility shall be considered by primary party organizations.

Decisions of party organizations to impose penalties on members or candidate members of these party committees, and on members of inspection commissions shall be taken in the usual manner.

Proposals of party organizations to expel from the CPSU shall be communicated to the respective party committee of which the given communist is a member. Decisions to expel from the party members or candidate members of the Central Committee of the communist party of a union republic or of a territorial, regional, area, city or district party committee, or members of an auditing commission, shall be taken at the plenary meeting of the respective committee by a majority of two-thirds of the vote of its members.

The question of expelling from the party a member or candidate member of the Central Committee of the CPSU or a member of the Central Auditing Commission, shall be decided by the party congress, and in the interval between two congresses, by the Plenum of the Central Committee, by a majority of two-thirds of the members of the Central Committee.

12. If a party member commits a criminally punishable offense, he shall be expelled from the party and shall be brought to responsibility in accordance with the law.

13. Appeals against expulsion from the party or against the imposition of a penalty, as well as decisions of party organizations to expel from the party, shall be considered by the appropriate party agencies within not more than one month from the date of their receipt.

CHAPTER II

Candidate Members of The Party

[text omitted]

CHAPTER III

Organizational Structure of The Party, Inner Party Democracy

19. The governing principle of the organizational structure of the party shall be democratic centralism, which signifies:

(a) Election of all leading party agencies, from the lowest to the highest;

(b) Periodic reports of party agencies to their party organizations and to higher bodies;

(c) Strict party discipline and subordination of the minority to the majority;

(d) Unconditional binding force of decisions of higher agencies upon lower agencies.

20. The party shall be built on the territorial-and-production principle: primary organizations shall be created at places of work of communists, and shall be united territorially in district, city, *etc.,* organizations. An organization serving a given area shall be higher than all party organizations serving part of that area.

CHAPTER IX

Party Groups in Non-Party Organizations

67. In congresses, conferences and meetings convoked by soviets, trade unions, cooperatives and other mass organizations of the working people, and also in elective agencies of these organizations, having not less than three party members, party groups shall be organized. The tasks of such groups shall be the all-around strengthening of the influence of the party and the carrying out of its policy among non-party people, the strengthening of party and state discipline, the struggle against bureaucratism, and the verification of the fulfillment of party and soviet directives.

68. Party groups shall be subordinate to the appropriate party agencies: The Central Committee of the Communist Party of the Soviet Union, the Central Committees of the communist parties of the union republics, the territorial, regional, area, city or district party committee.

In all questions party groups shall be obliged strictly and undeviatingly to abide by the decisions of the leading party agencies.

CHAPTER X

Party Funds

[text omitted]

III. STATUTE ON THE COMMITTEE OF PARTY-STATE CONTROL OF THE CENTRAL COMMITTEE OF THE COMMUNIST PARTY OF THE SOVIET UNION AND THE COUNCIL OF MINISTERS OF THE USSR AND ON THE CORRESPONDING LOCAL AGENCIES[1]

Enacted by Decree of the Central Committee of the Communist Party of the Soviet Union and the Council of Ministers of the USSR, December 20, 1962, SP SSSR, 1963, no. 1, item 1, as printed in A. I. Lepeshkin (general editor), *Sbornik ofitsial'nykh dokumentov po sovetskomu gosudarstvennomu pravu {Collection of Official Documents on Soviet State Law}* (Moscow, 1964), p. 180; and in *Spravochnik partiinogo rabotnika, Vypusk piatyi {Party Official's Handbook, Issue Five}* (Moscow 1964), p. 303.

NOTE: The Russian word *kontrol'* is translated here as "control," although it has the meaning of supervision or verification, rather than direction or regulation; *cf.* the German *Kontrolle* and the French *contrôle.*

I.

The correct organization of control and verification of performance is a most important Leninist principle of the activity of the Communist Party and the Soviet state in the construction of the new society, and a powerful means for improvement of party and state leadership, for the strengthening of the tie of the party with the people, for the attraction of the masses into the administration of the affairs of society. In proportion to the further movement of our country forward toward communism, to the complexity of the direction of economic construction, and to the gigantic development of productive forces, the role of mass control will grow still more and more.

In fulfillment of the directive of the Twenty-Second Congress of the CPSU, the November (1962) Plenum of the Central Committee of the CPSU adopted a decision on the radical reorganization of the system of control in the country, placing at its foundation the Leninist idea of the combination of party and state control, creating a system of single, all-embracing, permanently functioning control with the participation therein of the broad masses of communists and of all working people. V. I. Lenin saw in the flexible combination of the soviet and the party a guarantee of successful work, a source of extraordinary force for our policy.

Proceeding from this, the Central Committee of the CPSU, the Presidium of the Supreme Soviet of the USSR, and the Council of Ministers of the USSR have formed a single agency—the Committee of Party-State Control of the Central Committee of the CPSU and the Council of Ministers of the USSR (CPSC).

What is most important in the activity of the Committee of Party-State Control of the Central Committee of the CPSU and the Council of Ministers of the USSR,

---

1. A law of December 9, 1965, transformed the Committee of Party-State Control into the Committee of People's Control. *Vedomosti,* 1965, no. 49, item 719. The 1965 law provided for the issuance of a new statute to govern the Committee of People's Control. No copy of the new statute (if it has been issued) was available to the authors when the book went to press. The reorganization may have marked a return to the separation of Party and non-Party control agencies which existed before 1963. The breadth of inspection functions of the Communist Party, reflected in the 1962 statute here translated, was not intended to be diminished by the 1965 reform.

63

and of its local agencies, is the rendering of aid to the party and the state in the fulfillment of the Program of the CPSU, in the organization of systematic verification of actual fulfillment of directives of the party and the government, in the further improvement of direction of communist construction, in the struggle for the overall development of the socialist economy, in the observance of party and stat discipline and of socialist legality.

The agencies of party-state control must look deeply into our entire socialist economy, must be well informed on the state of affairs, and must give a correct, objective evaluation on the course of fulfillment of the party and the government.

The task of the control agencies is to be unswerving in their work by V. I. Lenin's instruction: *"Verify people and verify the actual performance of a thing—in this, yet again in this, and only in this is the clincher of all work and of all policy."*

Decisive conditions for the successful activity of the agencies of party-state control are: the most active and the broadest attraction both of the communist and the non-party masses, of women, of the youth, to the business of control; broad publicity in this work, realised through meetings of the working people, the press, radio, television, motion pictures; an attentive attitude toward letters and complaints, warnings, and proposals of Soviet people.

The agencies of party-state control shall act as practical organizers of mass public control, of the most democratic type, the likes of which are not known to a single capitalist state, where the working people are completely deprived of this right.

The committees of party-state control, being agencies of the party and of the state, shall not only verify and punish, but, chiefly, prevent mistakes and the possibility of any kind of abuses, shall help the Central Committee of the Communist Party of the Soviet Union and the Council of Ministers of the USSR to educate and warn cadres against shortcomings and blunders in their work, shall direct them toward the successful solution of political and economic tasks.

The committees of party-state control, the whole huge army of their activists, must construct their work in such a way that bureaucrats and red-tape artists, parasites, bribe-takers, thieves, speculators, and cheats [literally: spectacle-wipers] will sense the inevitability of punishment, will shudder before the great force of the Soviet public.

The agencies of party-state control must actively support, reward, and develop all the new, the advanced, and the progressive that arises in all spheres of our life, must decisively and persistently achieve the elimination of hidden shortcomings, must take real measures to ensure, as a result of verifications, the improvement of the state of affairs and the unconditional performance of the directives of the party and the government.

The assignment of these tasks to the agencies of party-state control shall not remove from party, soviet, and economic organizations responsibility for the verification of the fulfillment of decisions of the party and the government. On the contrary, it is necessary to increase the responsibility of party, soviet, economic, planning, and other agencies of the entire party and state apparatus from top to bottom for the organization of absolute fulfillment of the directives of the party and the government.

II.

1. The Committee of Party-State Control of the Central Committee of the CPSU and the Council of Ministers of the USSR, being a union-republican agency,

shall consist of a Chairman of the Committee, Deputy Chairmen, and members of the Committee, who shall be leading workers of the Committee and of local committees of party-state control, representatives of trade unions, of the Young Communist League, of the press, of workers, of collective farmers, and of the intelligentsia, who enjoy general trust.

The membership of the Committee shall be confirmed by the Central Committee of the CPSU and the Council of Ministers of the USSR, and the responsible workers of the Committee staff shall be confirmed by the Central Committee of the CPSU.

The Committee of Party-State Control shall realize all its activity under the direct guidance of the Central Committee of the CPSU and the Council of Ministers of the USSR and shall be accountable to them.

2. The republic, territorial (*krai*), and regional (*oblast'*) committees of party-state control shall be agencies of the communist party central committees and the councils of ministers of the union republics, of territorial and regional committees of the party, and of executive committees of territorial and regional soviets of working people's deputies.

The membership of the republican, territorial, and regional committees of party-state control shall include the leading workers of such committees, representatives of subordinate control agencies, of trade union and Young Communist League organizations, and of the press, and authoritative comrades from among workers, collective farmers, and intelligentsia.

In territories and regions where two independent territorial or regional committees of the party and two territorial or regional soviets of working people's deputies have been created, there shall be formed two committees of party-state control.

Republican, territorial, and regional committees of party-state control shall be confirmed at the plenary meetings of the respective party committees. The chairmen of the republican, territorial, and regional committees of party-state control and their deputies, shall be proposed by the Committee of Party-Sstate Control of the Central Committee of the CPSU and the Council of Ministers of the USSR and confirmed by the Central Committee of the CPSU and the Council of Ministers of the USSR.

The Committee of Party-State Control of the Bureau of the Central Committee of the CPSU for the RSFSR and the Council of Ministers of the RSFSR shall be confirmed by the Central Committee of the CPSU.

3. City and district committees of party-state control and committees of party-state control for collective and state farm production administrations and for industrial zones shall be agencies of republican, territorial, and regional committees of party-state control. The membership of the said committees shall be confirmed at plenary meetings of the respective party committees. The committees shall include representatives of trade union, Young Communist League, and other social organizations, and of the press, and authoritative comrades from among workers, collective farmers, and intelligentsia.

The chairmen of such committees shall be confirmed by superior party and control agencies and shall be an authorized representative of republican, territorial, and regional committees of party-state control.

4. At enterprises, construction sites, on collective and state farms, and in institutions and housing administrations there shall be formed groups for the assistance of committees of party-state control, by means of delegating to them

representatives from party, trade union, Young Communist League, and other social organizations, elected at meetings of such organizations as well as at general meetings of collective farmers and residents of housing adminitrations. The most active and authoritative comrades, both communist and non-party workers, collective farmers, specialists, employees, scholars, persons active in literature and art, pensioners, and housewives must be brought into the assistance groups. In the largest assistance groups, a group bureau may be elected.

The chairmen of the assistance groups and their deputies shall be elected at a general meeting of the members of the group and shall be confirmed by the party committee or bureau of the primary party organization and by the superior agency of party-state control.

In shops, departments, divisions and brigades of enterprises, construction projects, and collective and state farms there shall be formed groups or posts for the assistance of party-state control, from representatives delegated to their membership from party, trade union, and Young Communist League organizations and from meetings of collective farmers.

The assistance groups shall work under the guidance of party organizations and of appropriate local agencies of party-state control and shall be organizational centers about which shall be united all social control.

Assistant groups shall be granted a broad possibility for placing questions before administrations, party, trade union, and Youung Communist League organizations, and before committees of party-state control, concerning the elimination of short-comings discovered by them and concerning the bringing of the guilty to responsibility. The proposals of the assistance groups shall be considered by the directors of enterprises, of contruction projects, of collective farm, of state farms, and of institutions, and by primary party, trade union, and Young Communist League organizations.

Assistance groups shall periodically make reports on the work they have carried out at party, trade union, and Young Communist League meetings and meetings of the working people.

5. The Committee of Party-State Control of the Central Committee of the CPSU and the Council of Ministers of the USSR and its agencies shall directly, and in necessary instances jointly with the departments of the Central Committee of the CPSU, with the staff of the Council of Ministers of the USSR, and with local party committees and party and soviet organizations:

(a) Carry out a verification of the actual fulfillment of the directives of the party and the government by ministries, state committees, departments, organizations, enterprises, contruction projects, collective farms, state farms, and institutions;

(b) Control the fulfillment of the national economic plans, uncover internal reserves and unused possibilities for expanding production in industry and agriculture, for improving the quality of products, for reducing its cost, and for increasing the productivity of labor, carry on a struggle for the strictest regime of economy and for the correct and most expedient expenditure of means and of material valuables;

(c) Render aid to the party in the improvement of the work of the state and administrative apparatus, and in its further economization and improvement;

(d) Decisively suppress violations of party and state discipline, manifestations of localism, a departmental approach to affairs, cheating [literally, spectacle-wiping], falsification, mismanagement, and squandering;

(e) Wage a ruthless struggle against bureaucratism and red tape, bribery, speculation, abuse of official position, and against any infringements of socialist property; exercise control of the amount of work and the amount of consumption, for the observance of the socialist principle: "He who does not work, neither shall he eat;" speak out against any other actions that cause harm to the construction of communism;

(f) The Committees of Party-State Control of the Central Committee of the CPSU and of the Council of Ministers of the USSR shall place before the Central Committee of the CPSU and the Council of Ministers of the USSR questions having a general party and general state significance, on the basis of the generalized results of verifications of the fulfillment of the directives of the party and the government.

(6) The Committee of Party-State Control of the Central Committee of the CPSU and the Council of Ministers of the USSR and its local agencies shall have the right:

(a) To give to the appropriate administrators of ministries, state committees, departments, organizations, enterprises, construction projects, collective farms, and institutions, instructions concerning the elimination of shortcomings and violations in the fulfillment of decrees of the party and the government. The administrators of Soviet and economic organizations, enterprises, construction projects, collective farms, and institutions shall be obliged to eliminate without delay violations and shortcomings discovered by committees of party-state control and to report the results to appropriate agencies of party-state control.

(b) To hear reports, and to demand explanations as well as necessary documents and materials from administrators who badly fulfill the decrees and instructions of the party and the government, allowing bureaucratism and red tape; to impose penalties on persons guilty of presenting incorrect or false information and conclusions;

(c) To recommend to the appropriate agencies and organizations that reports of directors be heard by executive committees and at sessions of soviets of working people's deputies, collegia of ministries, state committees and departments, sessions of party committees, and at general meetings of workers, collective farmers, and employees, on questions connected with the elimination of shortcomings in the fulfillment of decrees of the party and the government;

(d) To suspend orders and actions of organizations, institutions, and officials that are illegal and could cause harm to the interests of the state;

(e) To set time limits for corrections by persons guilty of unsatisfactory fulfillment of decisions of the party and the government; in necessary instances to transfer cases for the consideration of comrades' courts, to assess monetary deficiencies against officials who have caused material harm to state, cooperative, or social organizations;

(f) To bring the guilty to responsibility, to impose disciplinary penalties, to reduce in official position, to dismiss from positions occupied, to refer materials on abuses and other criminal actions to the agencies of the procuracy for bringing the guilty to criminal responsibility.

The agencies of party-state control shall be obliged to use intelligently the rights presented to them, not to overbear in the application of penalties, but also not to spare those persons who by their actions bring harm to the business of constructing communism.

7. The committee of party-state control, from top to bottom, along with their staff, shall create auxiliary departments, permanent and temporary social commissions, shall have auxiliary inspectors and comptrollers, brought to the work

of the agencies of party-state control on the recommendation of party, soviet, and social organization.

The agencies of party-state control may invite to verifications, investigations, and audits, staff officials of party, soviet and economic agencies, of enterprises, construction projects, collective farms, state farms, institutions, and members of auditing commissions and control-auditing commission of the staff of ministries, state committees, and departments.

Republican, territorial, and regional committees of party-state control may invite for fulfillment of their tasks auxiliary workers, as a rule on a social service basis, but in necessary instances (on the basis of a special instruction confirmed by the Council of Ministers of the USSR) with release from basic work in production for a term of up to two weeks a year and with preservation of average monthly wages at the place of work.

The agencies of party-state control shall educate their staff and auxiliary workers, and the members of groups and posts for the assistance of committee of party-stat control, in the spirit of genuine Leninist qualities and traits of character and of high responsibility to the party and the state for the fulfillment of their honorable duties.

8. For the purposes of the wide publicity of their work, the agencies of party-state control shall actively use the press, motion pictures, radio, and television, shall systematically publish the results of verifications and of measures taken by them, and shall attract to the business of control worker and rural correspondents, journalists, writers, poets, artists.

IV. CODE OF CRIMINAL PROCEDURE OF THE RUSSIAN SOVIET FEDERATED SOCIALIST REPUBLIC, Adopted October 27, 1960,

As Amended to September 1, 1965 (Excerpts)

NOTE: The translation follows that of the full translation of the code by Harold J. Berman and James W. Spindler in Berman, *Soviet Criminal Law and Procedure: The RSFSR* (Cambridge, Mass., 1966).

SECTION ONE: GENERAL PROVISIONS

CHAPTER ONE

Fundamental Provisions

Article 1

Legislation on criminal proceedings. The method of conducting proceedings in criminal cases on the territory of the RSFSR shall be determined by the Fundamentals of Criminal Procedure of the USSR and the Union Republics, by other laws of the USSR promulgated in accordance therewith, and by the RSFSR Code of Criminal Procedure.

In the conduct of a criminal case the law of criminal procedure shall be applied which is in force at the time of the inquiry, preliminary investigation or judicial consideration of the case, respectively.

Regardless of the place where a crime has been committed, proceedings in criminal cases on the territory of the RSFSR shall in all instances be conducted in conformity with the RSFSR Code of Criminal Procedure.

The method of conducting judicial proceedings established by laws of criminal procedure shall be uniform and binding in all criminal cases and for all courts, agencies of the procuracy, of preliminary investigation and of inquiry.

Article 2 [text omitted]

Article 3

Obligation to initiate criminal case and expose a crime. A court, procurator, investigator and agency of inquiry shall be obliged, within the limits of their competence, to initiate a criminal case in every instance in which indicia of a crime are disclosed and to take all measures provided by law for ascertaining the event of the crime and the persons guilty of committing it, and for punishing them.

Articles 4-10 [text omitted]

Article 11

Inviolability of person. No one may be subjected to arrest except by decree of a court or with the sanction of a procurator.

A procurator shall be obliged to release immediately any person illegally deprived of freedom or kept under guard for more than a term provided for by law or by a judgment of a court.

Article 12

Inviolability of dwelling space and secrecy of correspondence. The inviolability of citizens' dwelling space and the secrecy of correspondence shall be protected by law.

Search where citizens live, impounding of correspondence and its seizure at postal and telegraph offices may be conducted only on the grounds and in accordance with the procedure established by law.

Article 13

Administration of justice only by courts. Justice in criminal cases shall be administered only by courts. No one may be deemed guilty of committing a crime or subjected to criminal punishment except by judgment of a court.

Articles 14-15 [text omitted]

Article 16

Independence of judges and their subordination only to law. In administering justice in criminal cases, judges and people's assessors shall be independent and subordinate only to law.

Judges and people's assessors shall decide criminal cases on the basis of law in conformity with socialist legal consciousness under conditions excluding outside pressure upon them.

Article 17 [text omitted]

Article 18

Publicity of judicial examination. The examination of cases in all courts shall be open, except in instances when this contradicts the interests of protecting a state secret.

In addition, a closed judicial examination shall be permitted, upon a reasoned ruling of the court, in cases of crimes of persons who have not attained the age of sixteen years, cases of sexual crimes, or other cases for the purpose of preventing the divulgence of information about intimate aspects of the lives of persons participating in the case.

The judgments of courts shall in all cases be proclaimed publicly.

Articles 19-32 [text omitted]

Article 33

Operation of law of criminal procedure with respect to citizens of foreign states and persons without citizenship. Judicial proceedings in cases of crimes committed by citizens of foreign states and by persons without citizenship shall be conducted on the territory of the RSFSR in conformity with the rules of the present Code.

With respect to persons possessing the right of diplomatic immunity, procedural actions provided for by the present Code shall be carried out only upon their request or with their consent. Consent for the carrying out of such actions shall be obtained through the Ministry of Foreign Affairs.

Article 34 [text omitted]

CHAPTER V

Evidence

Article 68

Circumstances subject to proof in criminal case. [text omitted]

Article 69

Evidence. [text omitted]

Article 70

Collection of evidence. A person conducting an inquiry, investigator, procurator and court shall have the right in cases conducted by them to summon, in accordance with the procedure established by the present Code, any person to be interrogated or to give an opinion as an expert; to conduct views, searches and other investigative actions provided for by the present Code; to demand that institutions, enterprises, organizations, officials and citizens furnish articles and documents capable of establishing factual data necessary for the case; and to demand that inspections be carried out.

Evidence may be presented by a suspect, accused, defense counsel and accuser, as well as by a victim, civil plantiff, and civil defendant and their representatives, and by any citizens, institutions, enterprises, and organizations.

All evidence collected in a case shall be subject to careful, thorough and objective verification on the part of a person conducting an inquiry, investigator, procurator, and court.

Article 71

Evaluation of evidence. [text omitted]

Article 72

Persons summoned as witnesses. [text omitted]

Article 73

Duties of witness. A witness shall be obliged to appear when summoned by a person conducting an inquiry, investigator, procurator, or court, and to give truthful testimony: to communicate everything known to him about the case and to reply to the questions put to him.

If a witness fails to appear without a valid reason, a person conducting an inquiry, investigator, procurator, or court shall have the right to subject him to compulsory appearance.

For refusing to give or evading the giving of testimony, a witness shall bear responsibility in accordance with Article 182 of the RSFSR Criminal Code; and for knowingly giving false testimony, in accordance with Article 181 of the RSFSR Criminal Code.

Article 74

Testimony of witness. [text omitted]

Article 75

Testimony of victim. [text omitted]

Article 76

Testimony of suspect. A suspect shall have the right to give testimony in connection with the circumstances which serve as the ground for his detention or confinement under guard, and also in connection with other circumstances of the case known to him.

Article 77

Testimony of accused. The accused shall have the right to give testimony concerning the accusation presented to him or in connection with any other circumstances of the case known to him or in connection with any other evidence in the case.

A confession of guilt by the accused may become the basis for an accusation only if the confession is confirmed by the totality of evidence in the case.

Article 78

Expert examination. [text omitted]

Article 79

Obligatory conduct of expert examination. [text omitted]

Article 80

Opinion of expert. [text omitted]

Article 81

Supplementary and repeated expert examination. [text omitted]

Article 82

Duties and rights of expert. [text omitted]

Article 83

Real evidence. [text omitted]

Article 84

Preserving real evidence. [text omitted]

Article 85

Measures taken with respect to real evidence when resolving criminal case. [text omitted]

Article 87

Records of investigative and judicial actions. [text omitted]

Article 88

Documents. [text omitted]

CHAPTER SIX

Measures of Restraint

Article 89

Application of measures of restraint. If there exist sufficient grounds for supposing that an accused will hide from an inquiry, preliminary investigation or court, or that he will hinder the establishment of the truth in a criminal case, or that he will engage in criminal activity, and also in order to secure the execution of a judgment, the person conducting the inquiry, investigator, procurator or court shall have the right to apply to the accused one of the following measures of restraint: signed promise not to depart, personal surety, surety of social organizations, confinement under guard.

With the sanction of the procurator or in accordance with a ruling of the court, bail may be applied as a measure of restraint.

Surveillance may be applied as a measure of restraint to members of the armed forces by the command of the military units in which they are serving.

In the absence of grounds necessitating the application of a measure of restraint, an obligation shall be obtained from the accused to appear when summoned and to give notice of a change of place of residence.

Article 90

Application of measure of restraint against suspect. In exceptional instances a measure of restraint may be applied against a person suspected of committing a crime even before presenting an accusation against him. In such instance the accusation must be presented not later than ten days from the moment of application of the measure of restraint. If in this period an accusation is not presented, the measure of restraint shall be cancelled.

CHAPTER EIGHT

Initiation of a Criminal Case

Article 108

Reasons and grounds for initiating criminal case. [text omitted]

Article 109

Requirement to consider declarations and communications concerning a crime. [text omitted]

Article 110

Declarations and communications concerning a crime. [text omitted]

Article 111

Giving oneself up. [text omitted]

Article 112

Procedure for initiating criminal case. If there exist a reason and grounds for initiating a criminal case, a procurator, investigator, agency of inquiry or judge shall be obliged, within the limits of their competence, to initiate a criminal case.

A procurator, investigator, agency of inquiry or judge shall render a decree to initiate a criminal case. The decree must indicate the time, place, by whom it is drawn up, the reason and grounds for initiating the case, the article of the criminal law in accordance with those indicia it is initiated, as well as the further routing of the case.

A copy of the decree to initiate a criminal case rendered by the investigator or agency of inquiry shall be sent immediately to the procurator.

Simultaneously with the initiation of a criminal case, measures must be taken to prevent or suppress the crime and to preserve the traces of the crime.

Article 113

Refusal to initiate criminal case. [text omitted]

Article 114

Referral of declaration or communication to another investigative or judicial jurisdiction. [text omitted]

Article 115

Referral of case after its initiation. [text omitted]

Article 116

Supervision of procurator over legality of initiation of criminal case. A procurator shall exercise supervision over the legality of the initiation of a criminal case.

If the case is initiated by an investigator or agency of inquiry without legal reasons and grounds, the procurator shall by his own decree vacate the decree of the investigator or agency of inquiry, thereby refusing to initiate the criminal case, or shall terminate the case if investigative actions have been conducted in it.

In the event of an unfounded refusal to initiate a case, the procurator shall by his own decree vacate the decree to such effect rendered by the investigator or agency of inquiry and shall initiate the case.

CHAPTER NINE

The Inquiry

Article 117

Agencies of inquiry. The following shall constitute agencies of inquiry:

(1) agencies of the police;

(2) commanders of military units and formations and heads of military institutions, in cases of all crimes committed by members of the armed forces subordinate to them as well as by persons subject to military service in their training courses, and in cases of crimes committed by workers and employees of the armed forces in connection with discharge of their occupational duties or within the purview of the unit, formation or institution;

(3) agencies of state security, in cases referred by law to their jurisdiction;

(4) heads of correctional labor institutions in cases of crimes against the established procedure for performance of service committed by persons working in such institutions, and in cases of crimes committed within the purview of correctional labor institutions;

(5) agencies of state fire supervision, in cases of causing fires and of violations of rules of fire prevention;

(6) agencies of border protection, in cases of violations of the state border;

(7) captains of ocean-going vessels on long voyages and heads of polar stations during periods of absence of transportation connections with the polar station.

Article 118

Duties of agencies of inquiry. Agencies of inquiry shall be charged with taking necessary operative-search measures and any other measures provided for by criminal-procedure law for the purpose of discovering crimes and the persons who have committed them.

Agencies of inquiry shall also be charged with the duty to take all measures necessary to prevent and suppress crime.

The activity of agencies of inquiry shall differ depending on whether they are acting in cases for which a preliminary investigation is obligatory or in cases for which a preliminary investigation is not obligatory.

Article 119

Activity of agencies of inquiry in cases for which preliminary investigation is obligatory. If there exist indicia of a crime for which a preliminary investigation is obligatory, an agency of inquiry shall initiate a criminal case, and, governed by the rules of criminal-procedure law, shall conduct urgent investigative actions to establish and preserve traces of the crime: view, search, seizure, examination, detention and interrogation of suspects, interrogation of victims and witnesses.

The agency of inquiry shall immediately inform a procurator of the discovery of the crime and of the commencement of the inquiry.

Upon performing urgent investigative actions, the agency of inquiry may conduct investigative and search actions in connection with it only upon the commission of the investigator. In the event that it transfers to the investigator a case in which it has not appeared possible to discover who committed the crime, the agency of inquiry shall continue to take operative-search measures to ascertain the criminal and shall inform the investigator of the results.

Article 120

Activity of agencies of inquiry in cases in which preliminary investigation is not obligatory. In cases in which a preliminary investigation is not obligatory, an agency of inquiry shall initiate the case and shall take all the measures provided by criminal-procedure law to establish the circumstances to be proved in the criminal case.

In an inquiry in a case for which a preliminary investigation is not obligatory, the agency of inquiry shall be governed by the rules established by the present Code for a preliminary investigation, with the following exceptions:

(1) defense counsel shall not participate in the inquiry;

(2) a victim, civil plaintiff, civil defendant and their representatives shall be notified of the completion of the inquiry and of referral of the case to a procurator, but the materials of the case shall not be presented to them for examination;

(3) the rules established by paragraph two of Article 127 of the present Code shall not apply to agencies of inquiry. When there is disagreement with a commission of a procurator, the agency of inquiry shall have the right to appeal from it to a higher procurator, without suspending execution of such commission.

In cases in which a preliminary investigation is not obligatory, the materials of the inquiry shall constitute the basis for consideration of the case in court.

Article 121

Period for conducting inquiry. In cases for which a preliminary investigation is obligatory, the inquiry must be completed not later than ten days from the day the case is initiated.

In cases in which a preliminary investigation is not obligatory, the inquiry must be completed not later than one month from the day the criminal case is initiated, including in this period the drawing up of a conclusion to indict or a decree to terminate or suspend the case.

The period of inquiry established by paragraph two of the present article may be prolonged by the procurator exercising immediate supervision over the inquiry, but not for more than one month.

In exceptional instances the period of the inquiry in a case may be prolonged in accordance with the rules established by Article 133 of the present Code.

Article 122

Detention of person suspected of committing crime. An agency of inquiry shall have the right to detain a person suspected of committing a crime for which punishment may be assigned in the form of deprivation of freedom, only if one of the following grounds exist:

(1) when such person is caught committing the crime or immediately after committing it;

(2) when eye-witnesses, including victims, directly indicate the given person as the one who has committed the crime;

(3) when obvious traces of the crime are discovered on the suspect or on his clothing, where he is, or in his dwelling.

If there exist other data that give grounds to suspect that a person has committed a crime, he may be detained only if he has attempted to flee or if he does not have a permanent place of residence or if the identity of the suspect has not been established.

An agency of inquiry shall be obliged to draw up a record of any instance of detaining a person suspected of committing a crime, with indication of the grounds and reasons for detention, and shall be obliged to give notice thereof to a procurator within twenty-four hours. The procurator shall be obliged, within forty-eight hours from the moment of receiving notification of a detention, to sanction confinement under guard or to free the person detained.

Article 123

Summons and interrogation of suspect. Summons and interrogation of a suspect shall be conducted in conformity with the rules established by Articles 145-147 and 150-152 of the present Code.

Before interrogation, a suspect's rights as provided by Article 52 of the present Code must be explained to him. It must be declared to him what crime he is suspected of committing, and a note to such effect must be made in the record of his interrogation.

If a suspect has been detained or a measure of restraint in the form of confinement under guard has been selected with respect to him, his interrogation shall be conducted immediately. If, however, it does not appear possible to conduct the interrogation immediately, the suspect must be interrogated not later than twenty-four hours from the moment of detention.

Article 124

Completing or suspending inquiry. In cases in which a preliminary investigation is not obligatory, the inquiry shall end with the drawing up of a decree to refer the case to an investigator.

In cases in which a preliminary investigation is not obligatory, the inquiry shall end with the drawing up of of a conclusion to indict or a decree to terminate the case. If there exists one of the grounds provided for by Article 208 of the present Code, the agency of inquiry shall terminate the case with a reasoned decree, a copy of which shall be sent to a procurator within twenty-four hours. In remaining instances a conclusion to indict shall be drawn up which, with all the materials of inquiry, shall be presented to the procurator for approval.

If there exists one of the grounds provided for by Article 195 of the present Code, the agency of inquiry shall have the right to suspend the conduct of a case in which a preliminary investigation is not obligatory. A decree shall be rendered to suspend the inquiry and a copy shall be sent to the procurator within twenty-four hours.

CHAPTER TEN

General Conditions for Conducting the Preliminary Investigation

Article 125

Agencies of preliminary investigation. Preliminary investigation in criminal cases shall be conducted by investigators of the procuracy, and also by investigators of agencies of protection of public order and investigators of agencies of state security.

Article 126

Requirement of preliminary investigation and investigative jurisdiction. [text omitted]

Article 127

Powers of investigator. [text omitted]

Article 128

Enlisting public to participate in exposing crimes. [text omitted]

Article 129

Commencement of preliminary investigation. [text omitted]

Article 130

Procedure for ruling on challenge of investigator. [text omitted]

Article 131

Requirement to grant petitions of significance for a case. [text omitted]

Article 132

Place of conducting preliminary investigation. [text omitted]

Article 133

Period for preliminary investigation. A preliminary investigation in a criminal case must be completed within a period of not more than two months. Such period shall include the time from the day of initiating the case until the moment the case is referred to the procurator with a conclusion to indict or with a decree to transfer the case to a court for consideration of the question of applying compulsory measures of a medical character or until the termination or suspension of the case.

The period for preliminary investigation established by paragraph one of the present article may be prolonged by a procurator of an autonomous republic, territory, region, autonomous region or national area, or by a military procurator of a military area or fleet, but not for more than two months. Further prolongation of the period for preliminary investigation may be carried out only in exceptional instances by the RSFSR Procurator, Chief Military Procurator, or USSR Procurator General.

When a court returns a case for supplementary investigation, or when a suspended or terminated case is reopened, the period for the supplementary investigation shall be established by the procurator who exercises supervision over the investigation, within limits of up to one month from the moment of acceptance of the case. Further prolongation of the period shall be carried out on the usual grounds.

In the event that it is necessary to prolong the period of the investigation, the investigator shall be obliged to draw up a reasoned decree to such effect and to present it to the appropriate procurator before the expiration of the period for preliminary investigation.

Article 134

Participation of interpreter. [text omitted]

Article 135

Participation of witnesses of investigative actions. [text omitted]

Article 136

Declaration as victim. [text omitted]

Article 137

Declaration as civil plaintiff. [text omitted]

Article 138

Prosecution as civil defendant. [text omitted]

Article 139

Impermissibility of divulging data of preliminary investigation. [text omitted]

Article 140

Measures to eliminate causes and conditions facilitating commission of crime. [text omitted]

Article 141

Record of investigative action. [text omitted]

Article 167

Grounds for conducting seizure. In the event that it is necessary to remove certain articles or documents of significance for a case, and if it is known precisely where they are and who has them, and investigator shall conduct a seizure.

The seizure of documents containing information which constitutes a state secret shall be conducted only with the sanction of a procurator and in accordance with a procedure agreed upon with the director of the respective institution.

Seizure shall be conducted in accordance with a reasoned decree of the investigator.

Article 168

Grounds for conducting search. If an investigator has sufficient grounds to suppose that the instruments of a crime, or articles or valuables criminally acquired, or other articles or documents which may be of significance for the case, are on some premises or in any other place or are in someone's possession, he shall conduct a search to find and remove them.

A search may also be conducted for finding wanted persons, as well as corpses.

A search shall be conducted in accordance with a reasoned decree of the investigator and only with the sanction of a procurator. In instances not permitting delay a search may be conducted without the sanction of a procurator, but the procurator must be informed subsequently within one day of the search.

Article 169

Persons present during seizure and search. The presence of witnesses of investigative actions shall be obligatory during the conduct of a seizure or search.

The presence of the person at whose dwelling place a search or seizure is conducted, or of adult members of his family, must be secured during the search or seizure. In the event that it is impossible for them to be present, representatives of the management of the apartment house or of the executive committee of the rural or settlement soviet of working people's deputies shall be invited.

Seizures or searches on premises occupied by institutions, enterprises, or organizations shall be conducted in the presence of a representative of the given institution, enterprises, or organization.

Persons at whose dwelling place a search or seizure is conducted, witnesses of investigative actions and representatives must be informed of their right to be present at all the actions of the investigator and to make statements for entry in the record that pertain to such actions.

Article 170

Procedure for conducting seizure and search. It shall not be permitted to conduct seizure or search at night, except in instances not permitting delay. In undertaking a seizure or search, an investigator shall be obliged to present a decree to such effect.

When conducting a seizure after presentation of a decree, the investigator shall propose that the articles or documents subject to removal be given up, and in the event of a refusal to do so shall conduct a compulsory seizure.

When conducting a search after presentation of a decree, the investigator shall propose that the instruments of the crime, articles and valuables criminally acquired, or other articles or documents which might be of significance for the case, be given up. If they are given up voluntarily and there are no grounds to fear the concealment of the articles and documents being sought, the investigator shall have the right to limit himself to removing what has been given up without conducting further explorations.

When conducting search and seizure the investigator shall have the right to open locked premises and storehouses if the owner refuses to open them voluntarily, but the investigator must avoid unnecessary damage to locks, doors, and other articles.

The investigator shall be obliged to take measures to prevent the public discloseure of circumstances of the intimate life of the person occupying the premises, or of other persons, which are revealed during search or seizure.

The investigator shall have the right to prohibit persons in the premises or place where the search is being conducted, as well as persons arriving at the premises or place, from leaving it or from communicating with one another or with any other persons until the completion of the search.

Article 171

Removal of articles and documents during seizure and search. When conducting seizure and search an investigator must be strictly limited to removing articles and documents which may have a relation to the case. Articles and documents prohibited from circulation shall be subject to removal regardless of their relation to the case.

All the removed articles and documents shall be presented to the witnesses of investigative actions and to other persons present and when necessary shall be packed and sealed at the place of the seizure or search.

Article 172

Personal search. Personal search shall be conducted in conformity with the rules of Articles 167-171 of the present Code.

Personal search may be conducted without rendering a separate decree to such effect and without the sanction of a procurator:

(1) during detention or confinement under guard;

(2) if there exist sufficient grounds to suppose that a person on the premises or in any other place where a seizure or search is being conducted is concealing on his person articles or documents which may be of significance for the case.

Personal search may be conducted only by a person of the same sex as the one being searched and in the presence of witnesses of investigative actions of the same sex as the one being searched.

Article 173

Conducting search and seizure on premises of diplomatic missions. Seizure and search may be conducted on premises occupied by diplomatic missions, or on premises in which members of diplomatic missions and their families live, only upon the request or with the consent of the diplomatic representative. The consent of the diplomatic representative to seizure or search shall be obtained through the Ministry of Foreign Affairs.

The presence of a procurator and of a representative of the Ministry of Foreign Affairs shall be obligatory in the conduct of a seizure or search on the said premises.

Article 174

Seizure of postal and telegraphic correspondence. Impounding of correspondence and its seizure at postal and telegraph offices may be carried out only with the sanction of a procurator or in accordance with a ruling or decree of a court.

When it is necessary to impound correspondence and to conduct a view and seizure of it, an investigator shall render a reasoned decree to such effect. After approval of the said decree by a procurator, the investigator shall refer the decree to the proper postal and telegraph office, shall propose that it hold the correspondence and shall notify it of the time of his arrival to view and seize the correspondence. The view and seizure shall be conducted in the presence of witnesses of investigative actions from among the employees of the postal and telegraph office.

Article 175

Impounding of correspondence shall be cancelled by decree of the investigator when there is no further necessity for the application of such measure.

Impounding of property. For the purpose of securing a civil suit or possible confiscation of property an investigator shall be obliged to impound property of an accused, a suspect or persons legally bearing material responsibility for their actions, or of other persons in possession of property criminally acquired.

Impounding of property may be carried out simultaneously with seizure or search, or independently.

The investigator shall draw up a reasoned decree to impound property. The property to be impounded shall be described in conformity with the rules of Articles 169 and 170 of the present Code. All the property described must be presented to the witnesses of investigative actions and other persons present.

Articles necessary for the accused himself or for persons dependent on him may not be impounded. The list of such articles is established by legislation of the RSFSR.

Impounded property shall be transferred for safekeeping, at the discretion of the investigator, to a representative of the executive committee of the rural or settlement soviet of working people's deputies, or to a representative of the management of the apartment house or to the owner of such property or a relative of his, or to any other person, and responsibility for the safekeeping of the property must be explained to such person and his signature to such effect must be obtained. When necessary the property which has been impounded may be removed.

When deposits of money are impounded the conduct of any operations in connection with them shall be terminated.

The impounding of property shall be cancelled by decree of the investigator if there is no further necessity for the application of such measure.

Article 176

Record of seizure, search, impounding of property. A record of a seizure, search or impounding of property shall be drawn up in conformity with the requirements of Articles 141 and 142 of the present Code. If in addition to the records a special inventory is drawn up of articles and documents removed or transferred for special safekeeping, the inventory shall be appended to the record. The record of the seizure, search or impounding of property must contain an indication that the rights provided by Article 169 of the present Code were explained to the persons present, and the statements made by them.

With respect to articles and documents subject to removal, it must be indicated whether they have been given up voluntarily or removed compulsorily, and in exactly what place and under what circumstances they have been discovered. All the articles and documents removed as well as all the property described must be enumerated in the record or the inventory appended to it, with a precise indication of quantity, size, weight, or individual indicia and as far as possible their value.

If in the seizure, inventory or impounding of property there have been attempts to destroy or hide articles and documents, or instances of breach of order on the part of the persons being searched or other persons, the record must contain an indication thereof and of the measures taken by the investigator.

Article 177

Obligation to hand over copy of record. A copy of the record shall be handed to, and a receipt obtained from, the person at whose dwelling place the seizure, search or impounding of property has been conducted, or adult members of the family, or in their absence, a representative of the executive committee of the rural or settlement soviet of working people's deputies or the management of the apartment house.

If the seizure, search or impounding of property has been conducted on premises belonging to an institution, enterprise or organization, a copy of the record shall be handed to the appropriate official and a receipt obtained from him.

CHAPTER EIGHTEEN
Supervision of the Procurator Over Execution Of the Laws in the Conduct of the Inquiry and The Preliminary Investigation

Article 211

Powers of procurator in exercising supervision over execution of laws in conduct of inquiry and preliminary investigation. A procurator shall exercise supervision over the execution of the laws in the conduct of an inquiry or a preliminary investigation in accordance with the USSR Statute on Procuratorial Supervision.

(1) The procurator shall be obliged:

(a) to institute criminal proceedings against persons guilty of commiting crimes, to take measures so that not a single crime remains undiscovered and not a single criminal escapes responsibility;

(b) strictly to see to it that not a single citizen is subjected to illegal or unfounded institution of criminal proceedings or any other illegal limitation of rights;

(c) to see to the undeviating observance of the procedure established by the present Code for conducting the inquiry and preliminary investigation;

(d) to exercise supervision so that no one is subjected to arrest otherwise than in accordance with a decree of a court or with the sanction of a procurator; in deciding the question of sanction for arrest the procurator shall carefully acquaint himself with all the materials upon which the arrest is founded and when necessary shall personally interrogate the accused or suspect.

(2) The procurator shall have the right:

(a) to give instructions concerning the conduct of the inquiry and preliminary investigation, concerning selection, change or cancellation of measures of restraint with respect to the suspect or accused, concerning prosecution of one as the accused, classification of the crime and scope of the accusation, and concerning referral of the case, as well as concerning individual investigative actions and search for criminals in hiding;

(b) to demand for verification, from an agency of inquiry or an investigator, criminal files, documents, materials, and other information concerning crimes committed and concerning the course of the inquiry, the preliminary investigation, and the search for criminals;

(c) to participate in the inquiry and preliminary investigation and when necessary to conduct personally a preliminary investigation or individual investigative actions in any case;

(d) to return criminal cases to the agency of inquiry or the investigator with his written instructions concerning supplementary investigation;

(e) to vacate illegal and unfounded decrees of the agency of inquiry or investigator;

(f) to remove the person conducting the inquiry or the investigator from further conduct of the inquiry or investigation if he has permitted the law to be broken in the investigation of a case;

(g) to withdraw any case from an agency of inquiry and transfer it to an investigator, or to transfer a case from one investigator to another, for the purpose of securing more complete and more objective investigation of the case;

(h) to entrust to agencies of inquiry the performance of individual investigative actions and measures of search in cases being conducted by investigators of agencies of the procuracy;

(i) to terminate criminal cases on grounds provided for by the present Code.

Article 212

Binding nature of procurator's instructions. [text omitted]

Article 213

Problems to be resolved by procurator in case received with conclusion to indict. [text omitted]

Article 214

Procurator's decision concerning case received with conclusion to indict. [text omitted]

Article 215

Change of accusation in procurator's confirmation of conclusion to indict. [text omitted]

Article 216

Change by procurator of measure of restraint or of list of persons subject to being summoned to judicial session. [text omitted]

Article 217

Referral of case to court by procurator. [text omitted]

CHAPTER NINETEEN

Appeal From Actions of the Agency of Inquiry, The Investigator and the Procurator

Article 218

Procedure for appeal. Appeals from actions of an agency of inquiry or an investigator shall be made to a procurator directly or else through the person conducting the inquiry or the investigator from whose actions an appeal is taken. Appeals may be both written and oral. Oral appeals shall be entered in the record, which shall be signed by the petitioner and by the person receiving the appeal.

The person conducting the inquiry or the investigator shall be obliged to refer an appeal that has been received to the procurator within twenty-four hours together with his explanation.

Until its resolution, the bringing of an appeal shall not suspend the execution of the action appealed from, if such is not found necessary by the person conducting the inquiry, the investigator or the procurator, as appropriate.

Article 219

Consideration of appeal by procurator. [text omitted]

Article 220

Appeal from actions and decisions of procurator. [text omitted]

V. CRIMINAL CODE OF THE RUSSIAN SOVIET FEDERATED

SOCIALIST REPUBLIC, Adopted October 27, 1960, As Amended to

September 1, 1965 (Excerpts)

NOTE: The translation follows that of the full translation of the code by Harold J. Berman and James W. Spindler in Berman, *Soviet Criminal Law and Procedure: The RSFSR Codes* (Cambridge, Mass., 1966).

GENERAL PART

CHAPTER ONE
General Provisions

Article 1

Tasks of RSFSR Criminal Code. The RSFSR Criminal Code has as its tasks the protection of the Soviet social and state system, of socialist property, of the person and rights of citizens, and of the entire socialist legal order, from criminal infringements.

For carrying out these tasks the RSFSR Criminal Code determines which socially dangerous acts are criminal, and establishes the punishments applicable to persons who have committed crimes.

Article 2

RSFSR Criminal Code and all-union criminal legislation. The RSFSR Criminal Code proceeds from the principles and general provisions established by the Fundamentals of Criminal Legislation of the USSR and union republics.

All-union laws concerning criminal responsibility for crimes against the state and military crimes and also all-union laws which determine responsibility for other crimes directed against the interests of the USSR shall be included in the present Code. Prior to inclusion of all-union criminal laws in th RSFSR Criminal Code they shall be directly applied on the territory of the RSFSR.

The General Part of the Code shall extend both to acts specified in the present Code and to acts for which responsibility is provided by all-union laws not yet included in the present Code.

Article 3

Basis of criminal responsibility. Only a person guilty of committing a crime, *i.e.,* who intentionally or negligently commits a socially dangerous act provided for by law, shall be subject to criminal responsibility and punishment.

Criminal punishment shall be applied only by judgment of a court.

CHAPTER TWO
Limits of Operation of Criminal Code

Article 4

Operation of present Code with respect to acts committed on territory of RSFSR. All persons who commit crimes on the territory of the RSFSR shall be subject to responsibility in accordance with the present Code.

In the event that crimes are committed on the territory of the RSFSR by diplomatic representatives of foreign states and other citizens who, in accordance with prevailing laws and international agreements, are not subject to criminal jurisdiction in Soviet judicial institutions, the question of their criminal responsibility shall be decided by diplomatic means.

Article 5

Operation of present Code with respect to acts committed outside boundaries of USSR. Citizens of the USSR who commit crimes abroad shall be subject to responsibility in accordance with the present Code if criminal proceedings are instituted against them or they are brought to trial on the territory of the RSFSR.

Persons without citizenship who are situated in the RSFSR and who have committed crimes beyond the boundaries of the USSR shall bear responsibility on the same basis.

If the persons specified in paragraphs one and two of the present article have undergone punishment abroad for the crimes committed by them, a court may accordingly mitigate the assigned punishment or may completely relieve the guilty person from serving the punishment.

For crimes committed by them outside the boundaries of the USSR, foreigners shall be subject to responsibility in accordance with Soviet criminal laws in instances provided for by international agreements.

Article 6

Operation of a criminal law in time. The criminality and punishability of an act shall be determined by the law prevailing at the time of the commission of that act.

A law eliminating the punishability of an act or reducing the punishment for it shall have retroactive force, that is, it shall extend also to acts committed before its promulgation.

A law establishing the punishability of an act or increasing the punishment for it shall not have retroactive force.

CHAPTER THREE

Crime

Article 7

The concept of crime. A socially dangerous act (an action or an omission to act) provided for by the Special Part of the present Code which infringes the Soviet social or state system, the socialist system of economy, socialist property, the person, or the political, labor, property or other rights of citizens, or any other socially dangerous act provided for by the present Code which infringes the socialist legal order, shall be deemed a crime.

Although an action or an omission to act formally contains the indicia of an act provided for by the Special Part of the present Code, it shall not be a crime, if by reason of its insignificance it does not represent a social danger.

Article 8

Intentional commission of a crime. [text omitted]

Article 9

Commission of crime through negligence. [text omitted]

Article 10

Responsibility of minors. [text omitted]

Article 11

Non-imputability. [text omitted]

Article 12

Responsibility for crime committed in state of intoxication. [text omitted]

Article 13

Necessary defense. [text omitted]

Article 14

Extreme necessity. [text omitted]

Article 15

Responsibility for preparation of crime and for attempted crime. [text omitted]

Article 16

Voluntary refusal to commit a crime. [text omitted]

Article 17

Complicity. [text omitted]

Article 18

Concealment. When not promised in advance, the concealment of a criminal as well as of instruments and means of committing a crime, of traces of a crime or of articles criminally acquired shall entail responsibility only in instances specially provided for by the Special Part of the present Code.

Article 19

Failure to report. Failure to report a crime reliably known to be in preparation or to have been committed shall entail criminal responsibility only in instances specially provided for by the Special Part of the present Code.

CHAPTER FOUR

Punishment

[text omitted]

CHAPTER FIVE

Assignment of Punishment and Relief from Punishment

[text omitted]

CHAPTER SIX
*Compulsory Measures of a Medical and
Educational Character*

[text omitted]

SPECIAL PART
CHAPTER ONE
Crimes Against the State

I. ESPECIALLY DANGEROUS CRIMES AGAINST THE STATE
Article 64

Treason. (a) Treason, that is, an act intentionally committed by a citizen of the USSR to the detriment of the state independence, the territorial inviolability or the military might of the USSR: going over to the side of the enemy, espionage, transmission of a state or military secret to a foreign state, flight abroad or refusal to return from abroad to the USSR, rendering aid to a foreign state in carrying on hostile activity against the USSR, or a conspiracy for the purpose of seizing power, shall be punished by deprivation of freedom for a term of ten to fifteen years with confiscation of property with or without additional exile for a term of two to five years, or by death with confiscation of property.

(b) A citizen of the USSR recruited by a foreign intelligence service for carrying on hostile activity against the USSR shall not be subject to criminal responsibility if he has committed no actions in execution of the criminal assignment received by him and has voluntarily reported to agencies of authority his connection with the foreign intelligence service.

Article 65

Espionage. Transfer or the stealing or collection for purpose of transfer to a foreign state or foreign organization or its secret service, of information constituting a state or military secret, or transfer or collection on assignment from a foreign intelligence service of any other information for use to the detriment of the interests of the USSR, if the espionage is committed by a foreigner or person without citizenship, shall be punishable by deprivation of freedom for a term of seven to fifteen years, with confiscation of property, with or without additional exile for a term of two to five years, or by death with confiscation of property.

Article 66

Terrorist act. The killing of a state or social figure or representative of authority, committed in connection with his state or social activity, for the purpose of undermining or weakening the Soviet authority, shall be punished by deprivation of freedom for a term of ten to fifteen years with confiscation of property, with or without additional exile for a term of two to five years.

Article 67

Terrorist act against representative of foreign state. The killing of a representative of a foreign state for the purpose of provoking war or international complications shall be punished by deprivation of freedom for a term of ten to fifteen years with confiscation of property, with or without additional exile for a term of two to five years, or by death with confiscation of property.

Grave bodily injury caused to the same persons for the same purpose shall be punished by deprivation of freedom for a term of eight to fifteen years with confiscation of property, with or without additional exile for a term of two to five years.

Article 68

Sabotage. The destruction or damaging, by explosion, arson, or other means, of enterprises, structures, routes and means of transportation, means of communications or other state or social property, or the commission of mass poisoning or the spreading of epidemics or epizootics, for the purpose of weakening the Soviet state, shall be punished by deprivation of freedom for a term of eight to fifteen years with confiscation of property, with or without additional exile for a term of two to five years, or by death with confiscation of property.

Article 69

Wrecking. An action or omission to act directed toward the undermining of industry, transport, agriculture, the monetary system, trade or other branches of the national economy, or the activity of state agencies or social organizations, for the purpose of weakening the Soviet state, if such act is committed by making use of state or social institutions, enterprises, or organizations, or by obstructing their normal work, shall be punished by deprivation of freedom for a term of eight to fifteen years with confiscation of property, with or without additional exile for a term of two to five years.

Article 70

Anti-Soviet agitation and propaganda. Agitation or propaganda carried on for the purpose of undermining or weakening Soviet authority or of committing particular especially dangerous crimes against the state, or circulating for the same purpose slanderous fabrications which defame the Soviet state and social system, or circulating or preparing or keeping, for the same purpose, literature of such content, shall be punished by deprivation of freedom for a term of six months to seven years, with or without additional exile for a term of two to five years, or by exile for a term of two to five years.

The same actions committed by a person previously convicted of especially dangerous crimes against the state or committed in wartime shall be punished by deprivation of freedom for a term of three to ten years, with or without additional exile for a term of two to five years.

Article 71

Propagandizing of war. The propagandizing of war, in whatever form it is conducted, shall be punished by deprivation of freedom for a term of three to eight years, with or without additional exile for a term of two to five years.

Article 72

Organizational activity directed to commission of especially dangerous crimes against the state and also participation in anti-Soviet organizations. Organizational activity directed to the preparation or commission of especially dangerous crimes against the state, or to the creation of an organization which has as its purpose the commission of such crimes, or participation in an anti-Soviet organization, shall be punished in accordance with Articles 64-71 of the present Code.

Article 73

Especially dangerous crimes against the state committed against another working people's state. By virtue of the international solidarity of working people, especially dangerous crimes against the state committed against another working people's state shall be punished in accordance with Articles 64-72 of the present Code.

90

II. OTHER CRIMES AGAINST THE STATE

Article 74

Violation of equality of rights of nationalities and races. [text omitted]

Article 75

Divulgence of state secret. Divulgence of information has been entrusted or has become known because of his position or work, in the absence of the indicia of treason or espionage, shall be punished by deprivation of freedom for a term of two to five years.

The same act, if it has resulted in serious consequences, shall be punished by deprivation of freedom for a term of five to eight years.

Article 76

Loss of documents containing state secrets. The loss of documents containing state secrets, or of article information concerning which constitutes a state secret, by a person to whom they have been entrusted, if the loss is a result of violation of the rules established for handling the aforementioned documents or articles, shall be punished by deprivation of freedom for a term of one to three years.

The same act, if it has caused serious consequences, shall be punished by deprivation of freedom for a term of three to eight years.

Article 77

Banditry. [text omitted]

Article 77-1

Actions disrupting work of correctional labor institutions. [text omitted]

Article 78

Smuggling. Smuggling, that is, illegal transfer of goods or other valuables across the state border of the USSR, committed by concealment of articles in special containers or by fraudulent utilization of customs or other documents, or on a large scale, or by a group of persons organized for engaging in smuggling, or by an official by utilization of his official position, or the smuggling of explosives, narcotics, virulent and poisonous substances, arms and military equipment, shall be punished by deprivation of freedom for a term of three to ten years with confiscation of property, with or without additional exile for a term of two to five years.

Article 79

Mass disorders [text omitted]

Article 80

Evasion of regular call to active military service. Evasion of a regular call to active military service shall be punished by deprivation of freedom for a term of one to three years.

The same act committed by means of causing oneself bodily injury or by malingering, by means of forgery of documents or by any other deception, or committed under other aggravating circumstances, shall be punished by deprivation of freedom for a term of one to five years.

Article 81

Evasion of call-up by mobilization. Evasion of a call-up by mobilization into the ranks of the Armed Forces of the USSR shall be punished by deprivation of freedom for a term of three to ten years.

The same act, or evasion of further calls for making up the complement of the Armed Forces of the USSR, committed in wartime, shall be punished by deprivation of freedom for a term of five to ten years or by death.

Articles 82

Evasion in wartime of fulfillment of compulsory service or payment of taxes. Evasion in wartime of labor mobilization or of fulfillment of other compulsory service, or of payment of taxes, shall be punished by deprivation of freedom to one year.

Article 83

Illegal exit abroad and illegal entry into the USSR. Exit abroad, entry into the USSR, or crossing the border without the requisite passport or the permission of the proper authorities, shall be punished by deprivation of freedom for a term of one to three years.

Operation of the present articles shall not extend to instances of arrival in the USSR of foreign citizens, without the requisite passport or permit, for exercise of the right of asylum granted by the Constitution of the USSR.

Article 84

Violation of rules of international flights. Flying into the USSR or out of the USSR without the requisite permit, nonobservance of the routes, landing places, air gateways, or height of flights indicated on the permit, or any other violation of rules of international flights, shall be punished by deprivation of freedom for a term of one to ten years or by a fine in an amount of not more than one thousand rubles with or without confiscation of the aircraft.

Article 85

Violation of rules of safe movement and operation of transport. Violation by a worker of rail, water or air transport of rules of safe movement and operation of transport, resulting in accidents involving persons, a wreck, damage or other serious consequences, or improper repair of means of transport, routes, or means of signaling and communication, resulting in such consequences, shall be punished by deprivation of freedom for a term of three to fifteen years.

The same acts, if they do not result in such consequences but create a known threat that such consequences will occur, shall be punished by deprivation of freedom for a term of one to three years or by correctional tasks for a term of up to one year.

Article 86

Damaging routes of communication and means of transport. The intentional destruction or damaging of routes of communication, structures thereon, rolling stock or vessels, means of communication or of signaling, which results in or could result in a train wreck, damage to a ship or interference with the normal operation of transport and communication, shall be punished by deprivation of freedom for a term of three to fifteen years, with or without additional exile for a term of two to five years.

Article 87

Making or passing counterfeit money or securities. [text omitted]

Article 88

Violation of rules on currency transactions. [text omitted]

Article 88-1

Failure to report crimes against the state. The failure to report crimes against the state that are known to be in preparation or to have been committed, provided for by Articles 64 (treason), 65 (espionage), 66 and 67 (terrorist act), 68 (sabotage), 69 (wrecking), 72 (organizational activity directed at commission of especially dangerous crimes against the state or participation in anti-Soviet organization), 77 banditry), 87 (making or passing counterfeit money or securities) of the present Code, shall be punished by deprivation of freedom for a term of one to three years or by correctional tasks for a term of six months to one year.

Article 88-2

Concealment of crimes against the state. When not promised in advance the concealment of crimes against the state provided for by Articles 64 (treason), 65 (espionage), 66 and 67 (terrorist act), 68 (sabotage), 69 (wrecking), 72 (organizational activity directed at commission of especially dangerous crimes against the state or participation in an anti-Soviet organization), 77 (banditry), 78 (smuggling), 87 (making or passing counterfeit money or securities), 88 violation of rules on currency transactions) of the present Code, shall be punished by deprivation of freedom for a term of one to five years with or without additional exile for a term of two to five years, or by exile for a term not exceeding five years.

CHAPTER TWO

Crimes Against Socialist Property

[text omitted]

CHAPTER THREE

Crimes Against Life, Health, Freedom and Dignity of the Person

[text omitted]

CHAPTER FOUR

Crimes Against Political and Labor Rights Of Citizens

[text omitted]

CHAPTER FIVE

Crimes Against Personal Property of Citizens

[text omitted]

CHAPTER SIX

Economic Crimes

Article 152

Issuing poor-quality, non-standard or incomplete products. [text omitted]

Article 152-1

Additions to and other distortions of accounts concerning fulfillment of plans. Additions to state accounts or the presentation of other intentionally distorted accounting data concerning the fulfillment of plans, as anti-state actions inflicting harm on the national economy of the USSR, shall be punished by deprivation of freedom for a term not exceeding three years.

Article 153

Private entrepreneurial activity and activity as commercial middleman. Private entrepreneurial activity and activity by utilization of state, cooperative or other social forms shall be punished by deprivation of freedom for a term not exceeding five years with confiscation of property or by exile for a term not exceeding five years with confiscation of property.

Activity as a commercial middleman carried on by private persons as a form of business for the purpose of enrichment shall be punished by deprivation of freedom for a term not exceeding three years with confiscation of property.

Article 154

Speculation. Speculation, that is, the buying up and reselling of goods or any other articles for the purpose of making a profit shall be punished by deprivation of freedom for a term not exceeding two years with or without confiscation of property, or by correctional tasks fr a term not exceeding one year, or by a fine not exceeding three hundred rubles.

Speculation as a form of business or on a large scale shall be punished by deprivation of freedom for a term of two to seven years with confiscation of property.

Petty speculation committed by a person who has previously been convicted of speculation shall be punished by deprivation of freedom for a term not exceeding one year or by correctional tasks for the same term or by a fine not exceeding two hundred rubles with confiscation of the articles of speculation.

Article 154-1

Buying up for feeding to cattle or poultry, or feeding to cattle or poultry, bread and other grain products. [text omitted]

Article 155

Illegal use of trademarks. [text omitted]

Article 156

Deception of purchasers. [text omitted]

Article 157

Issuing for sale poor-quality, non-standard and incomplete goods. [text omitted]

Article 158

Illegally making, supplying and storing alcoholic beverages. [text omitted]

Article 159

Forgery of marks of postal payment and of transportation tickets. [text omitted]

Article 160

Violation of veterinary rules. [text omitted]

Article 162

Engaging in a prohibited trade. Engaging in a trade concerning which there is a special prohibition, if such act does not entail administrative liability or if it is committed after imposition of an administrative penalty for such act, shall be punished by correctional tasks for a term not exceeding one year or by a fine not exceeding two hundred rubles.

Engaging in a trade concerning which there is a special prohibition, committed on a significant scale or by using hired labor, or committed by a person previously convicted of engaging in a prohibited trade, shall be punished by deprivation of freedom for a term not exceeding four years with or without confiscation of property.

Article 163

Illegally engaging in fishing and other water extractive trades. [text omitted]

Article 164

Illegally engaging in hunting of seals and beavers. [text omitted]

Article 165

Floating timber or blasting in violation of rules for protection of fish reserves. [text omitted]

Article 166

Illegal hunting. [text omitted]

Article 167

Violation of rules for mining and surrender of gold to the state. [text omitted]

Article 168

Intentional damage to crops by grazing and injury to plantings sheltering fields and other plantings. [text omitted]

Article 169

Illegally felling trees. [text omitted]

CHAPTER SEVEN

Official Crimes

Article 170

Abuse of authority or of official position. [text omitted]

Article 171

Exceeding authority or official powers. Exceeding authority or official powers, that is, the intentional commission by an official of actions clearly exceeding the limits of rights and powers granted to him by law, thereby causing substantial harm to state or social interests or to legally protected rights and interests of citizens, shall be punished by deprivation of freedom for a term not exceeding three years, or by correctional tasks for a term not exceeding one year, or by dismissal from office.

Exceeding authority or official powers, if accompanied by force, by use of weapons or by actions which torment the victim and insult his personal dignity, shall be punished by deprivation of freedom for a term not exceeding ten years.

Article 172

Neglect. The nonperformance or improper performance by an official of his duties as the result of a wrongful or unconscientious attitude toward them, causing substantial harm to state or social interests or to legally protected rights and interests of citizens, shall be punished by deprivation of freedom for a term not exceeding three years or by deprivation of freedom for a term not exceeding three years or by correctional tasks for a term not exceeding one year or by dismissal from office.

Article 173

Taking of bribe. [text omitted]

Article 174

Giving of bribe. [text omitted]

Article 174-1

Acting as intermediary in bribery. [text omitted]

Article 175

Official forgery. [text omitted]

CHAPTER EIGHT

Crimes Against Justice

Article 176

Institution of criminal proceedings against person known to be innocent. The institution of criminal proceedings against a person known to be innocent by a person conducting an inquiry, by an investigator, or by a procurator, shall be punished by deprivation of freedom for a term not exceeding three years.

The same actions combined with an accusation of an especially dangerous crime against the state or any other grave crime or with artificially created proof of the accusation shall be punished by deprivation of freedom for a term of three to ten years.

Article 177

Rendering of judgment, decision, ruling, or decree known to be unjust. [text omitted]

Article 178

Arrest or detention known to be illegal. Arrest known to be illegal shall be punished by deprivation of freedom for a term not exceeding one year.

Detention known to be illegal shall be punished by correctional tasks for a term not exceeding one year or by dismissal from office.

Article 179

Compulsion to give testimony. Compelling the giving of testimony by means of application of threats or other illegal actions on the part of a person conducting an inquiry or preliminary investigation shall be punished by deprivation of freedom for a term not exceeding three years.

The same actions combined with the application of force or with humiliation of the person interrogated shall be punished by deprivation of freedom for a term of three to ten years.

Article 180

Knowingly making false report. Knowingly making a false report of the commision of a crime shall be punished by deprivation of freedom for a term not exceeding three years or by correctional tasks for a term not exceeding one year.

The same actions combined with an accusation of an especially dangerous crime against the state or any other grave crime or with artificially created proof of the accusation, or committed for a mercenary purpose, shall be punished by deprivation of freedom for a term of two to seven years.

Article 181

Knowingly giving false testimony. The giving of testimony, known to be false, by a witness or by the victim, or of an opinion known to be false, by an expert, or of a translation by an interpreter which he knows to be incorrect and which is made by the interpreter in court or in the conduct of a preliminary investigation or inquiry, shall be punished by deprivation of freedom for a term not exceeding one year or by correctional tasks for the same term.

The same actions combined with an accusation of an especially dangerous crime against the state or any other grave crime or with artificially created proof of the accusation, or committed for a mercenary purpose, shall be punished by deprivation of freedom for a term of two to seven years.

Article 182

Refusal or evasion by witness or victim to give testimony or by expert to give opinion. The refusal or evasion by a witness or victim to give testimony or by an expert to give an opinion in a judicial session or in the conduct of a preliminary investigation or inquiry, or obstructing the appearance of a witness or victim or the giving of testimony by him, shall be punished by correctional tasks for a term not exceeding six months or by a fine not exceeding fifty rubles or by social censure.

Article 183

Compulsion of witness or victim to give false testimony or of expert to give false opinion, or bribery of such persons. Compelling a witness, victim or expert to give judicial or investigative agencies false testimony or a false opinion, committed by threatening such persons or their near ones with homicide, force, or destruction of property, or bribing a witness, victim or expert for the purpose of inducing him to give false testimony or a false opinion, shall be punished by deprivation of freedom for a term not exceeding two years or by correctional tasks for a term not exceeding one year.

Article 184

Divulgence of findings of preliminary investigation or inquiry. The divulgence of data of a preliminary investigation or inquiry without permission of the procurator, investigator or person conducting the inquiry shall be punished by correctional tasks for a term not exceeding six months or by a fine not exceeding fifty rubles.

Article 185

Embezzlement, alienation or concealment of property subjected to distraint or impounding. The embezzlement, alienation, or concealment of property subjected to distraint or impounding, committed by a person to whom such property is entrusted, shall be punished by deprivation of freedom for a term not exceeding one year or by correctional tasks for the same term.

Article 186

Escape from place of exile. [text omitted]

Article 187

Unwarranted return to a place forbidden for residence by one who has been banished. [text omitted]

Article 188

Escape from place of confinement or from custody. [text omitted]

Article 189

Concealment of crimes. When not promised in advance, the concealment of crimes provided for by articles [numbers and captions of articles omitted] of the present Code, shall be punished by deprivation of freedom for a term not exceeding five years or by correctional tasks for a term not exceeding one year.

The same act with respect to crimes provided for by articles [numbers and captions of articles omitted] of the present Code, shall be punished by deprivation of freedom for a term not exceeding two years or by correctional tasks for a term not exceeding one year.

Article 190

Failure to report crimes. Failure to report known crimes which are being prepared or have been committed, provided for by articles [numbers and captions of articles omitted] of the present Code, shall be punished by deprivation of freedom for a term not exceeding three years or by correctional tasks for a term not exceeding one year.

CHAPTER NINE

Crimes Against the System of Administration

Article 191

Resisting representative of authority or representative of public fulfilling duties of protection of public order. Resisting a representative of authority while he is performing duties entrusted to him by law, or resisting a representative of the public who is fulfilling duties for protection of public order, or compelling such person to carry out clearly illegal actions, committed by force or by threat of application of force, except in instances indicated in Article 191-1 of the present Code, shall be punished by deprivation of freedom for a term not exceeding three years or by correctional tasks for a term not exceeding one year or by a fine not exceeding sixty rubles.

Article 191-1 to Article 192-1

[text omitted]

Article 193

Threat or force against official or social worker. A threat of homicide, of infliction of grave bodily injuries, or of destruction of property by arson, against an official or a social worker, made for the purpose of terminating official or social activity, or of changing its character in the interests of the person making the threat, shall be punished by deprivation of freedom for a term not exceeding eight months or by correctional tasks for a term not exceeding one year or by social censure.

The infliction of light bodily injury or of beatings, or the commission of any other forcible actions against an official or a social worker in connection with his official activity or fulfillment by him of his social duty, shall be punished by deprivation of freedom for a term not exceeding three years or by correctional tasks for a term not exceeding one year.

Article 194

[text omitted]

Article 195

Stealing or damaging documents, stamps, seals or forms. [text omitted]

Article 196

Forging, making or supplying forged documents, stamps, seals, forms. [text omitted]

Article 197

Violation of rules of entry into or of living in frontier region or frontier zone. [text omitted]

Article 198

Violation of passport rules. [text omitted]

Article 198-1

[text omitted]

Article 199

Unwarranted seizure of land and unwarranted construction. [text omitted]

Article 200 and Article 201

[text omitted]

Article 202

Illegal use of insignia of Red Cross or Red Crescent. [text omitted]

[text omitted]

Article 203 to Article 205

[text omitted]

CHAPTER TEN

*Crimes Against Public Security, Public Order and
Health of the Population*

Article 206 to Article 210

[text omitted]

Article 211

Violation of rules of safe movement or operation of motor transport or urban electrical transport. The violation by a motor transport or urban electrical transport worker of rules of safe movement of transport, causing the victim less grave or light bodily injury or causing substantial material loss, shall be punished by deprivation of freedom for a term not exceeding two years or by correctional tasks for a term not exceeding one year with or without deprivation of the right to drive transport vehicles for a term not exceeding two years, or by a fine not exceeding one hundred rubles.

The same actions resulting in the death or grave bodily injury of the victim shall be punished by deprivation of freedom for a term not exceeding ten years with or without deprivation of the right to drive transport vehicles for a term not exceeding three years.

Article 212

Violation of rules of safe movement of transport by person not a motor transport worker. The violation of rules of safe movement of motor transport by a person not a motor transport worker, causing the victim less grave or light bodily injury, shall be punished by deprivation of freedom for a term not exceeding two years or by correctional tasks for a term not exceeding one year with or without deprivation of the right to drive motor vehicles for a term not exceeding three years.

The same actions resulting in the death or grave bodily injury of the victim shall be punished by deprivation of freedom for a term not exceeding ten years with or without deprivation of the right to drive motor vehicles for a term up to three years.

Article 213

Violation of rules governing transport. The violation of rules governing transport for the protection of order and safety of movement, resulting in the loss of human life or other grave consequences, shall be punishd by deprivation of freedom for a term not exceeding five years.

Article 214

Violation of rules for mining safety. [text omitted]

Article 215

Violation of rules when carrying on construction work. [text omitted]

Article 216

Violation of rules of safety in enterprises or shops where there is danger of explosion. [text omitted]

Article 217

Violation of rules for keeping, utilizing, registering or transporting explosives and radioactive materials. The violation of rules for keeping, utilizing, registering or transporting explosives and radioactive materials, or the illegal sending of such materials by post or carrier, if such actions could result in grave consequences, shall be punished by deprivation of freedom for a term not exceeding one year or by correctional tasks for the same term.

The same actions resulting in grave consequences shall be punished by deprivation of freedom for a term not exceeding seven years.

Article 218

Illegally carrying, keeping, making or supplying arms or explosives. Carrying, keeping, making or supplying a firearm (except a smooth-bore hunting piece), ammunition or explosives without an appropriate permit, shall be punished by deprivation of freedom for a term not exceeding one year, or by a fine not exceeding one hundred rubles.

Carrying, making or supplying daggers, Finnish daggers, or any other cutting weapon without an appropriate permit, except in those localities where the carrying of a cutting weapon is an accessory of the national costume or is connected with hunting, shall be punished by deprivation of freedom for a term not exceeding one year or by correctional tasks for the same term or by a fine not exceeding thirty rubles.

Article 219

Wrongfully keeping firearm. Wrongfully keeping a firearm, thereby creating conditions for use of such weapon by another person, resulting in grave consequences, shall be punished by deprivation of freedom for a term not exceeding one year or by correctional tasks for the same term.

Article 220

Illegally sending easily flammable or caustic materials. [text omitted]

Article 221

[text omitted]

Article 222

Violation of rules established for the purpose of combating epidemics. [text omitted]

Article 223

Pollution of water or air. [text omitted]

Article 224

Making or supplying narcotics or other virulent or poisonous substances. [text omitted]

Article 225 to Article 228

[text omitted]

Article 229

Desecration of grave. [text omitted]

Article 230

Intentionally destroying, demolishing or damaging cultural monuments. [text omitted]

CHAPTER ELEVEN

Crimes Constituting Survivals of Local Customs

[text omitted]

CHAPTER TWELVE

Military Crimes

Article 237

Concept of military crime. Crimes provided for by the present Code against the established procedure for performing military service, committed by persons in military service, or by persons subject to military service during training courses, shall be deemed to be military crimes.

Officers, noncommissioned officers and rank-and-file personnel of agencies of state security, as well as persons with respect to whom special indication is made in legislation of the USSR, shall bear responsibility for crimes against the established procedure for performing service in accordance with appropriate articles of the present Code.

Article 238

Insubordination.

(a) Insubordination, that is, openly refusing to execute an order of a superior or any other intentional failure to execute an order, shall be punished by deprivation of freedom for a term of one to five years.

(b) The same act committed by a group of persons or resulting in grave consequences shall be punished by deprivation of freedom for a term of three to ten years.

(c) Insubordination committed in wartime or in a combat situation shall be punished by death or by deprivation of freedom for a term of five to ten years.

Article 239

Failure to execute order. [text omitted]

Article 240

Resisting superior or compelling him to violate official duties. [text omitted]

Article 241

Threatening a superior. [text omitted]

Article 242

Forcible actions against superior. [text omitted]

Article 244

Insult by forcible action inflicted by one person in military service on another in absence between them of relationship of subordination or seniority. [text omitted]

Article 245 to Article 249

[text omitted]

Article 250

Dissipation {promotanie} or loss of military property. [text omitted]

Article 251

Intentional destruction or damaging of military property. [text omitted]

Article 252 to Article 258

[text omitted]

Article 259

Divulgence of military secret or loss of document containing military secret.

(a) Divulgence of information of a military character constituting a state secret, in the absence of the indicia of treason, shall be punished by deprivation of freedom for a term of two to five years.

(b) The loss of documents containing information of a military character constituting a state secret, or of articles information concerning which constitutes a state secret, by a person to whom such documents or articles have been entrusted, if the loss is a result of violation of the rules established for handling the aforementioned documents or articles, shall be punished by deprivation of freedom for a term of one to three years.

(c) Acts provided for by subsection "a" and "b" of the present article, resulting in grave consequences, shall be punished by deprivation of freedom for a term of five to ten years.

(d) Divulgence of military information not subject to disclosure but not constituting a state secret shall be punished by deprivation of freedom for a term of five to ten years.

(e) An act provided for by subsection "d" of the present article under mitigating circumstances shall entail the application of the rules of the Disciplinary Code of the Armed Forces of the USSR.

Article 260

Abuse of authority, exceeding authority and neglectful attitude toward duty.

[text omitted]

Article 261 to Article 269

[text omitted]

VI. FUNDAMENTAL PRINCIPLES OF CIVIL PROCEDURE OF THE USSR AND THE UNION REPUBLICS, Adopted by the Supreme Soviet of the USSR December 8, 1961 (Excerpts)

NOTE: Full English translations are printed in *Soviet Civil Legislation and Procedure, Official Texts and Commentaries* (Moscow, [1964?]), pp. 146-175, and (by Albert Kiralfy) in University of Leyden, *Law in Eastern Europe,* no. 7 (Leyden, 1963), pp. 299-317.

CHAPTER VI

The Civil Procedural Rights of Foreign Citizens and Persons Without Citizenship. Suits Against Foreign States, Judicial Commissions and Judgments of Foreign Courts. International Treaties and Agreements

Article 59

Civil procedural rights of foreign citizens and of foreign enterprises and organizations. Foreign citizens shall have the right to resort to the courts of the USSR and shall enjoy civil procedural rights equally with Soviet citizens.

Foreign enterprises and organizations shall have the right to resort to the courts of the USSR and shall enjoy civil procedural rights for the defense of their interests.

The Council of Ministers of the USSR may establish retaliatory restrictions with with respect to citizens, enterprises, and organizations of those states in which there are allowed special limitations upon the civil procedural rights for the defense of their interests.

The Council of Ministers of the USSR may establish retaliatory restrictions with respect to citizens, enterprises, and organizations of those states in which there are allowed special limitations upon the civil procedural rights of Soviet citizens, enterprises, or organizations.

Article 60

Suits against foreign states. Diplomatic immunity. The presentation of a suit against a foreign state, the securing of a suit and the attachment of property of a foreign state located in the USSR, may be allowed only with the consent of the competent agencies of the particular state.

Diplomatic representatives of foreign states who are accreditd to the USSR and other persons specified in relevant laws and international agreements shall be subject to the jurisdiction of a Soviet court in civil cases only within the limits determined by the norms of international law or by agreements with the particular states.

In those instances when, in a foreign state, the same judicial immunity which, in accordance with the present Article, is accorded to foreign states, their property or the representatives of foreign states in the USSR, is not accorded to the Soviet state, its property, or the representatives of the Soviet state, the Council of Ministers of the USSR or other authorized agency may prescribe the application of retaliatory measures upon that state, its property, or the representatives of that state.

Article 62

Execution of judicial commissions of foreign courts and presentation of commissions to foreign courts by courts of the USSR. The courts of the USSR shall execute commissions of foreign courts, transmitted to them in the established procedure, for the carrying out of individual procedural actions (service of process and of other documents, interrogation of parties and witness, carrying out of expert examination and view of the scene, *etc.*), with the exception of instances when:

(1) execution of the commission would contradict the sovereignty of the USSR or threaten the security of the USSR;

(2) execution of the commission is not within the competence of the court.

Execution of commissions of foreign courts for the carrying out of individual procedural actions shall be carried out on the basis of Soviet legislation.

The courts of the USSR may resort to foreign courts with commissions for the execution of individual procedural actions. The procedure for the relations of Soviet courts with foreign courts shall be determined by legislation of the USSR and the union republics and by international agreements of the USSR and the union republics.

Article 63

Execution in the USSR of decisions of foreign courts and arbitral tribunals. [text omitted]

Article 64

International treaties and agreements. In those instances when an international agreement to which the USSR is a party establishes rules other than those contained in the present Fundamental Principles, the rules of the international treaty or international agreement shall be applied.

The same principle shall be applied on the territory of a union republic, if an international treaty or international agreement to which the union republic is a party establishes rules other than those provided by the civil procedure legislation of the union republic.

VII. FUNDAMENTAL PRINCIPLES OF CIVIL LEGISLATION OF THE USSR AND THE UNION REPUBLICS, Adopted by the Supreme Soviet of the USSR, December 8, 1961. (Excerpts)

NOTE: Full English translations are printed in *Soviet Civil Legislation and Procedure, Official Texts and Commentaries* (Moscow, [1964?]), pp. 55-112 aand (by Albert Kiralfy) in University of Leyden, *Law in Eastern Europe*, No. 7 (Leyden, 1963), pp. 263-298.

Article 88

General foundations of liability for causing harm. Harm caused to the person or property of a citizen and also harm caused to an organization shall be subject to compensation in full by the person who has caused the harm.

The person who has caused the harm shall be freed from compensating for it if he proves that the harm was not caused by his fault.

An organization shall be obliged to compensate for harm caused by the fault of its employees in the performance of their labor (service) duties.

Harm caused by lawful actions shall be subject to compensation only in instances provided for by law.

Article 90

Liability for harm caused by a source of increased danger. Organizations and citizens whose activity is connected with increased danger to those nearby (transport organizations, industrial enterprises, construction sites, owners of automobiles, *etc.*) shall be obliged to compensate for harm caused by a source of increased danger, unless they prove that the harm arose as a consequence of an insuperable force or of the intent of the victim.

Article 122

Civil legal capacity of foreign citizens. Foreign citizens shall enjoy in the USSR civil legal capacity equally with Soviet citizens. Individual exceptions may be established by a law of the USSR.

The Council of Ministers of the USSR may establish retaliatory restrictions with respect to citizens of those states in which there are special restrictions on the civil legal capacity of Soviet citizens.

Article 129

International treaties and agreements. If an international treaty or international agreement to which the USSR is a party establishes rules other than those which are contained in Soviet civil legislation, then the rules of the international treaty or international agreement shall be applied.

The same principle shall be applied on the territory of a union republic, if an international treaty or international agreement to which the union republic is a party establishes rules other than those provided by the civil legislation of the union republic.

VIII. ON THE PROCEDURE FOR THE PUBLICATION AND ENTRY INTO FORCE OF LAWS OF THE USSR, DECREES OF THE SUPREME SOVIET OF THE USSR, AND EDICTS AND DECREES OF THE PRESIDIUM OF THE SUPREME SOVIET OF THE USSR, Edict of the Presidium of the Supreme Soviet of the USSR, June 19, 1958, *Vedomosti*, 1958, no. 14, item 275, as amended by a decree of March 11, 1960, which is reported but not published verbatim in *Vedomosti*, 1960, no. 13, pp. 125-126.[1]

For purposes of putting in order the matter of publication of the laws of the USSR and the edicts of the Presidium of the Supreme Soviet of the USSR and of clarifying the time periods of their entry into force, the Presidium of the Supreme Soviet of the USSR decrees:

1. It shall be established that laws of the USSR and decrees and other acts of the Supreme Soviet of the USSR are subject to publication in the "Vedomosti Verkhovnogo Soveta SSSR" [Gazette of the Supreme Soviet of the USSR—transl.] not later than seven days after their adoption.

2. The most important of the acts indicated in Article 1, which are subject to wide and immediate promulgation, shall be published in the newspaper "Izvestiia Sovetov deputatov trudiashchikhsia SSSR" [The formal title of the Soviet newspaper *Izvestia*—transl.]

In necessary instances these acts may be promulgated also by radio or transmitted by telegraph.

3. Edicts and decrees of the Presidium of the Supreme Soviet of the USSR not having general significance or not having a normative character shall be sent to the appropriate departments and institutions and brought by them to the attention of the persons to whom the effect of such acts extends. They may be left unpublished by decision of the Presidium of the Supreme Soviet of the USSR.

4. Treaties, agreements and conventions concluded by the USSR with foreign states and ratified in the established manner, and corresponding edicts on ratification, shall be published in "Vedomosti" on request of the Ministry of Foreign Affairs of the USSR to the Presidium of the Supreme Soviet of the USSR.

5. Laws of the USSR, decrees, and other acts of the Supreme Soviet of the USSR, and edicts and decrees of the Presidium of the Supreme Soviet of the USSR of a general normative character shall enter into force simultaneously on the whole territory of the USSR on the expiration of ten days after their publication in "Izvestia" or in "Vedomosti", unless in the acts themselves another term is indicated for putting them into force; such acts published in accordance with Article 2 of the present Edict in "Izvestia" before publication in "Vedomosti" shall enter into force on the expiration of ten days after publication in "Izvestia."

All other acts not having a general normative character shall enter into force from the moment of their adoption, unless in the acts themselves another term is indicated for putting them into effect.

6. Edicts and decrees of the Presidium of the Supreme Soviet of the USSR which are left unpublished in accordance with Article 3 of the present Edict shall enter into force from the moment of their receipt by the appropriate departments and institutions, unless in the acts themselves another term is indicated for putting them into effect.

1. A decree of September 3, 1965, provided for resumption of centralized publication of legislative materials in the languages of the union republics, a practice discontinued after the 1960 decree. *Vedomosti*, 1965, no. 36, item 515.

7. In connection with the issuance of the present Edict:

(a) [Repeal of prior legislation. Text omitted]

(b) The Council of Ministers of the USSR shall be commissioned to establish the procedure for the publication and entry into force of decrees and resolutions of the Council of Ministers of the USSR.

8. The present Edict shall be presented for confirmation by the Supreme Soviet of the USSR.

IX. ON THE PROCEDURE FOR THE PUBLICATION AND ENTRY INTO FORCE OF DECREES AND REGULATIONS OF THE GOVERNMENT OF THE USSR, Decree of the Council of Ministers of the USSR, March 30, 1959, SP SSSR, 1959, no. 6, item 37, as printed in *Sbornik normativnykh materialov po voprosam vneshnei torgovli SSSR, Vypusk 1 {Collection of Normative Materials on the Foreign Trade of the USSR, Issue 1}* (Moscow, 1961), p. 50.

The Council of Ministers of the USSR decrees:

1. It shall be established that decrees of the government of the USSR having general significance or having a normative character shall be published in the "Sobranie postanovlenii Pravitel'stva SSSR" [Collection of Decrees of the Government of the USSR—transl.] issued by the Managing Department of the Council of Ministers of the USSR.

Decrees of the government of the USSR which in view of their importance or the immediacy of the measures provided in them are subject to wide and immediate promulgation shall be published in the newspapers and in necessary instances shall be announced also on the radio or transmitted by telegraph.

2. It shall be established that in decrees of the government of the USSR of a normative character there should be indicated the time period for bringing them into force.

In those instances when the time period for bringing into force is not indicated in decrees of the government of the USSR, they shall enter into force from the moment of their adoption.

3. Regulations of the Council of Ministers of the USSR shall enter into force from the moment of their adoption and are not subject to publication in the "Sobranie postanovlenii Pravitel'stva SSSR."

4. Treaties, agreements, and conventions concluded by the USSR with foreign states and not subject to ratification, and also the corresponding decrees of the government on their confirmation, shall be published in the "Sobranie postanovlenii Pravitel'stva SSSR" upon the proposal of the Ministry of Foreign Affairs of the USSR.

5. Decrees of the government of the USSR not published in the "Sobranie postanovlenii Pravitel'stva SSSR" or in newspapers, and also regulations of the Council of Ministers of the USSR may be published in other printed publications upon the proposal of the appropriate organizations only with the permission of the Managing Department of the Council of Ministers of the USSR.

6. On the original copies of decrees of the government of the USSR subject to publication in accordance with paragraph 1 of the present decree the following superscriptions shall be made:

"Subject to publication in the Collection of Decrees;"

"Subject to publication in the Collection of Decrees and in the newspapers;"

"Subject to publication in the Collection of Decrees and in newspapers and to announcement by radio."

7. Decrees of the government of the USSR, independently of their publication in accordance with the present decree, shall be distributed by the Managing Department of the Council of Ministers of the USSR, immediately after their adoption, to the councils of ministers of the union republics, to the state committees of the Council of Ministers of the USSR, to the ministries of the USSR, to the Commission of Soviet Control of the Council of Ministers of the USSR [suc-

ceeded by the Committee of People's Control—transl.], to the **Procuracy of** the USSR, to the Supreme Court of the USSR, to the State Bank of the USSR, to the Central Statistical Administration of the USSR, to the **Committee** on State Security attached to the Council of Ministers of the USSR, and also to other organizations on a list designated by the Managing Department of the Council of Ministers of the USSR.

X. ON ESTABLISHING A LIST OF INFORMATION SUBJECT TO STATE SECRECY, DIVULGENCE OF WHICH IS PUNISHED BY LAW, Decree of the Council of Ministers of the USSR, April 26, 1956, *Ugolovnyi Kodeks RSFSR {Criminal Code of the RSFSR}* (Moscow, 1957), pp. 143-145.

The Council of Ministers of the USSR decrees:

There shall be established the following list of information subject to state secrecy:

INFORMATION OF A MILITARY CHARACTER

1. Mobilization plans and other documents containing collected information concerning the preparation for mobilization of the country as a whole, or of the armed forces, of the branches of the armed services, of the military districts, of the armies, the fleets and the flotillas, and also of all-union and union-republican ministries of the USSR and of enterprises of union significance.

2. Collected information concerning places of storage, stockpiles, and plans for stockpiling of all types of state and mobilization reserves and also of certain types of products having a defense or strategic significance, for the USSR as a whole, and for the Chief Administration of State Material Reserves attached to the Council of Ministers of the USSR and its territorial administrations.

3. Operative plans and collected information concerning the location and number of troops, the amount of armaments and military equipment for the armed forces as a whole, branches of the armed services, military districts, armies, fleets, and flotillas.

4. Generalized information concerning the military preparedness of troops and the state of discipline for the Ministry of Defense of the USSR as a whole, the Ministry of Internal Affairs of the USSR, branches of the armed services, military districts and fleets.

5. Collected information concerning the number under reserve military obligation for the USSR as a whole and for the military districts, and also information on the recruitment of troops through regular draft calls for the armed forces of the USSR as a whole, military districts, and fleets.

6. Plans with descriptions, sketches, and photographs of fortified regions, naval bases, central and district bases, and stocks of arms and ammunition, and also information on their armaments and equipment.

7. Collected information concerning the network of airports and the quality and capacity of airports for the USSR as a whole.

Collected information concerning defense, airport, base, and special construction for the armed forces as a whole, military districts and fleets.

8. Plans of preparation for local air defense of cities and of major industrial, defense, and special objectives.

9. Information concerning the condition of the defense of state borders.

INFORMATION OF AN ECONOMIC CHARACTER

10. Collected information concerning the location of enterprises of the munitions/war industry, concerning their production capacities, and concerning plans for production of armaments, military equipment, and ammunition, and information on the fulfillment of such plans in concrete terms, for the USSR as a whole, for all-union and union-republican ministries, for chief administrations, and for enterprises of union significance.

11. Collected information concerning production capacity and plans of production of non-ferrous, precious, and rare metals and reports of their fulfillment for the USSR as a whole, for the Ministry of Non-ferrous Metallurgy of the USSR, the Ministry of Non-ferrous Metallurgy of the Kazakh SSR, and their chief administrations.

12. Information concerning underground reserves in the USSR of radioactive elements, their extraction, production capacity, plans of production of radioactive and trans-uranium elements, and information concerning the fulfillment of the plans in absolute figures for the USSR as a whole, ministries, chief administrations and enterprises.

13. Information concerning the extent of underground reserves of non-ferrous, rare, and precious metals, titanium, diamonds, and piezo-optic minerals for the USSR as a whole, ministries and major deposits and also petroleum as a whole for the Ministry of the Petroleum Industry of the USSR.

14. Discoveries and inventions having major military significance.

Discoveries and inventions of major scientific and economic significance, prior to the grant of permission for their publication by the heads of ministries and departments.

15. The condition of foreign exchange reserves, information on the balance of payments, collected information concerning state reserves and places of safe-keeping of precious metals and precious stones for the USSR as a whole.

16. State codes.

17. Other information that may be added by the Council of Ministers of the USSR to the list of matters subject to state secrecy.

In connection with the publication of the present decree it shall be considered that the decree of the Council of Ministers of the USSR of June 8, 1947, no. 2009, "On establishing a list of information subject to state secrecy, divulgence of which is punished by law" has lost its force.

XI. ON THE PROCEDURE FOR RELATIONS OF STATE INSTITUTIONS OF THE USSR AND THEIR OFFICIALS WITH INSTITUTIONS AND OFFICIALS OF FOREIGN STATES, Edict of the Presidium of the Supreme Soviet of the USSR, December 16, 1947, *Vedomosti,* 1948, no. 5, p. 2, col. 3.

For the purposes of introducing a unified procedure in the relations of state institutions of the USSR and their officials with institutions and officials of foreign states, the Presidium of the Supreme Soviet of the USSR decrees:

1. It shall be established that relations of state institutions of the USSR and their officials with institutions and officials of foreign states located abroad shall be conducted through the Ministry of Foreign Affairs of the USSR.

The Ministry of Foreign Trade of the USSR and agencies subject to its control or persons authorized by it within the limits of their competence, shall deal directly in matters of trade relations with institutions and officials of foreign states located abroad.

Any other procedure of relations can obtain not otherwise than with direct authorization thereof in a law or in an international treaty of the USSR which has taken effect or by special permission of the Ministry of Foreign Affairs of the USSR.

2. It shall be established that relations of state institutions of the USSR and their officials with diplomatic representations of foreign states located on the territory of the USSR shall be carried out through the Ministry of Foreign Affairs or directly, the latter only with its consent.

The Ministry of Foreign Trade of the USSR and agencies subject to its control or persons authorized by it, within the limits of their competence, shall deal directly in matters of trade relations with embassies and missions of foreign states located on the territory of the USSR and also with their commercial counsellors and commercial attaches.

The Ministry of Foreign Trade of the USSR shall immediately inform the Ministry of Foreign Affairs of the USSR of all major questions of a political commercial nature arising in relations of this type.

The procedure for relations of economic organizations that have the right of independent access to foreign markets with commercial counsellors and commercial attaches of representations of foreign states located on the territory of the USSR shall be established by the Ministry of Foreign Trade of the USSR in coordination with the Ministry of Foreign Affairs of the USSR.

3. The procedure for relations of the high command of the Armed Forces of the USSR with foreign military and naval attaches present on the territory of the USSR shall be established by the Council of Ministers of the USSR on the representation of the Ministry of the Armed Forces of the USSR and the Ministry of Foreign Affairs of the USSR.

4. The procedure for relations of state institutions of the USSR and their officials with consular representations of foreign states present on the territory of the USSR shall be established by the Ministry of Foreign Affairs of the USSR on the basis of the laws of the USSR and international treaties of the USSR in force.

5. State institutions of the USSR and their officials, in an instance of receipt of any sort of written communications from institutions and officials of foreign states or from diplomatic representatives of foreign states present on the territory of the USSR, must send such communications, together with the necessary materials

on the merits of the question dealt with in the communication, to the Ministry of Foreign Affairs of the USSR or, in questions of trade relations, to the Ministry of Foreign Trade of the USSR. The answer to institutions or officials of foreign states with respect to their communications will be given by the Ministry of Foreign Affairs of the USSR or the Ministry of Foreign Trade of the USSR, as appropriate.

In instances of personal communications on the part of officials or institutions of foreign states of foreign diplomatic representations present on the territory of the USSR, the state institutions of the USSR and their officials must, without going into the consideration of the question on its merits, limit themselves to the explanation that officials of institutions of foreign states must communicate in accordance with the established procedure directly with the Ministry of Foreign Affairs of the USSR, and, on questions of trade relations, with the Ministry of Foreign Trade of the USSR. State institutions of the USSR and their officials must inform the Ministry of Foreign Affairs of the USSR or the Ministry of Foreign Trade of the USSR of facts of communications of this type.

6. The procedure for relations established in Article 5 of the present Edict shall not apply to institutions and officials in relations of an everyday nature, namely: at postal and telegraph institutions, windows and offices of railroad, city, water and air transport, customs offices, the police, notarial offices, housing administrations at the place of residence of the foreigners, fire departments, first-aid stations, stores and kiosks, including book stores, restaurant, enterprises for providing everyday services to the public, entertainment enterprises, museums, exhibits, and information bureaus—within the limits of the performance of their usual functions by the respective institutions and persons.

7. For violation of the procedure for relations of state institutions of the USSR and their officials with institutions and officials of foreign states, established by the present Edict, officials of state institutions of the USSR shall be subject to responsibility in criminal or disciplinary proceedings.

8. It shall be considered that the Decree of the Central Executive Committee and Council of People's Commissars of the USSR of August 27, 1926, "On the Procedure for Relations of Government Institutions and Officials of the USSR and the Union Republics with Government Institutions and Officials of Foreign States" SZ USSR, no. 58, item 426), has lost its force.

9. It shall be delegated to the presidia of the supreme soviets of the union republics to establish, in accordance with the present Edict, the procedure for relations of state institutions of the union republics and their officials with institutions and officials of foreign states.

XII. STATUTE ON DIPLOMATIC AND CONSULAR REPRESENTA-TIONS OF FOREIGN STATES ON THE TERRITORY OF THE USSR, May 23, 1966, *Vedomosti,* 1966, no. 22, item 387.

GENERAL PROVISIONS
Article 1.

A diplomatic representation (embassy or mission), and also a consular representation (consulate general, consulate, vice-consulate, or consular agency) on the territory of the USSR shall be granted, as agencies of foreign states, the privileges and immunities specified in the present Statute for the performance of their functions defined in accordance with a norms of international law. Privileges and immunities shall also be granted to the personnel of these representations to the extent provided by the following articles.

Article 2.

All persons enjoying the privileges and immunities specified in the present Statute shall be obliged to respect the laws, decrees, and rules in force in the USSR and the union republics.

Article 3.

In those instances when an international treaty in which the USSR participates establishes rules other than those which are contained in the present Statute, the rules of the international treaty shall be applied.

Article 4.

The present Statute shall extend (correspondingly) to diplomatic and consular representations of foreign states which may be opened on the territory of the union republics by agreement of these republics with foreign states.

DIPLOMATIC REPRESENTATIONS
Article 5.

The head of a diplomatic representation with the status of ambassador or minister shall be accredited to the Presidium of the Supreme Soviet of the USSR; with the status of chargé d'affaires—to the Ministry of Foreign Affairs of the USSR.

The accrediting state must receive consent (agrément) to the appointment of a given person as head of the diplomatic representation.

Article 6.

Counselors, trade representatives, army, navy, and air attachés, first, second, and third secretaries, attachés [and] secretary-archivists shall constitute members of the diplomatic staff of a representation. Deputy trade representatives [and] assistants of army, navy, and air attaches shall also be included in the diplomatic staff of a representation.

Consent must be obtained through diplomatic channels to the appointment of a given person as army, navy, or air attaché.

Article 7.

Premises occupied by a diplomatic representation shall be inviolable. Access to them may take place only with the consent of the head of the diplomatic representation or of a person substituting for him.

Such premises and the property situated in them, and also the means of transport of the representation, shall enjoy immunity from all coercive actions, including search, seizure, and attachment.

The residence of the head of the diplomatic representation and the housing premises of the members of the diplomatic staff shall enjoy the same inviolability and protection as the premises of the representation.

The inviolability of the above-mentioned premises and means of transport shall not give, however, the right to use them for purposes incompatible with the functions of the diplomatic representation.

Article 8.

The flag of the accrediting state may be flown, and its emblem displayed, on the premises of a diplomatic representation and on the residence of the head of the diplomatic representation.

The flag of the accrediting state may also be flown on the means of transportation of the head of the diplomatic representation.

Article 9.

A diplomatic representation may communicate without hindrance with its government, with consular representations of its country situated on the territory of the USSR, and also with diplomatic and consular representatives of its country in third states, by ordinary means of communication, by enciphered telegrams, and also by diplomatic mail. The representation may install radio transmitters and use them only with the permission of competent agencies of the USSR.

Th archives, documents, and official correspondence of a diplomatic representation shall be inviolable.

Diplomatic mail may neither be opened nor detained. All pieces constituting diplomatic mail must have visible external marks indicating their nature, and they may contain only diplomatic documents and items meant for official use.

The procedure for admitting diplomatic mail across the state border of the USSR shall be defined by rules issued by the Ministry of Foreign Trade and agreed upon with the Ministry of Foreign Affairs of the USSR and the Ministry of Finance of the USSR.

A diplomatic courier shall enjoy personal inviolability in the performance of his duties; he may not be subjected to arrest or detention.

The appropriate agencies of the USSR and the union republics shall render to diplomatic couriers all possible assistance to assure their unhindered movement to their destination and the safe-keeping of the diplomatic mail carried by them.

The provisions of the present article shall be applied also to temporary diplomatic ocuriers, appointed to carry only specific diplomatic mail (ad hoc diplomatic couriers). The immunities granted to temporary diplomatic couriers shall cease at the moment when they deliver the diplomatic mail to its destination.

On the basis of a special agreement with a foreign state, diplomatic mail may be sent by ordinary channels of communications unaccompanied by a courier, or may be entrusted to the captain of a civil airplane, who shall not be considered a diplomatic courier. The representation may send its employee to receive the diplomatic mail directly from the captain of the airplane.

Article 10.

The diplomatic representation shall be freed, on the basis of reciprocity, from all general public and local taxes and assessments.

This exemption shall not apply to payment for concrete types of service.

Article 11.

A diplomatic representation may, in accordance with the legislation of the USSR and with rules in effect in the USSR, import into the USSR items meant for official use, and the head of the diplomatic representation and members of the diplomatic staff of the representation [may import] items meant for their personal use.

Items meant for official use of the representation shall be exempt from customs duties. Items meant for the personal use of the head of the diplomatic representation and the members of the diplomatic staff of the representation, including items of initial supply, shall also enjoy exemption from customs duties.

The procedure for admitting the above-mentioned items across the state border of the USSR, and also for freeing them from payment of customs duties and from customs inspection, shall be defined by rules issued by the Ministry of Foreign Trade with the agreement of the Ministry of Foreign Affairs of the USSR and the Ministry of Finance of the USSR.

Article 12.

The head of a diplomatic representation and the members of the diplomatic staff of the representation shall enjoy personal inviolability. They may not be subjected to detention or arrest.

Articlue 13.

The head of a diplomatic representation and the members of the diplomatic staff of the representation shall enjoy immunity from the criminal, civil and administrative jurisdiction of the USSR and the union republics. However, such persons may be subjected to the jurisdiction of the USSR and the union republics in the event that consent thereto is clearly expressed by the accrediting state.

Immunity from civil jurisdiction shall not extend to instances when the head of a diplomatic representation and the members of the diplomatic staff enter into civil-law relations as private persons in connection with suits concerning structures belonging to them on the territory of the USSR, concerning inheritance, or concerning activity carried out by them outside the limits of their official functions.

The head of a diplomatic representation and the members of the diplomatic staff of the representation shall not be obliged to give testimony as witnesses, and in the event of consent to give such testimony they shall not be obliged to appear therefore in judicial or investigatory agencies.

Article 14.

The head of a diplomatic representation and the members of the diplomatic staff of the representation shall be freed, on the basis of reciprocity, from all general public and local taxes and assessments, and also from all personal duties.

Exemption from taxes and assessments shall not apply to payment for concrete types of services.

Article 15.

The privileges and immunities provided in Articles 11-14 of the present Statute shall extend to the members of the family of the head of the representation and also to the members of families of the diplomatic staff of the representation if the members of the family live together with the above-mentioned persons and are not Soviet citizens.

Article 16.

Employees of the administrative and technical staff of a diplomatic representation and members of their families living together with them, if such employees and members of their families are not Soviet citizens or do not live permanently in the USSR, shall enjoy, on the basis of reciprocity, the privileges and immunities provided in Article 7 (with respect to housing premises occupied by them) and in Articles 12-14 of the present Statute, with the exception that immunity from the civil and administrative jurisdiction of the USSR and the union republics shall extend only to actions performed by employees of the administrative and technical staff in fulfillment of their official duties.

Such persons shall also enjoy the customs exemptions with respect to items of initial supply.

On the basis of a special agreement with a foreign state, other privileges and immunities granted by the present Statute to members of a diplomatic staff may also be extended to the above-mentioned administrative and technical staff employees, proceeding with respect to each individual state from the principle of reciprocity.

Article 17.

Employees of the service staff of a diplomatic representation who are not Soviet citizens, or who do not live in the USSR permanently, shall enjoy, on the basis of reciprocity, the immunity provided by Article 13 of the present Statute with respect to actions performed by them in the fulfillmnt of official duties, and also exemption from taxes and assessments on wages received at their place of duty and from all personal duties. Members of their families living together with them, if they are not Soviet citizens or do not live in the USSR permanently, shall enjoy, on the basis of reciprocity, exemption from all personal duties.

On the basis of a special agreement with a foreign state, other privileges and immunities granted by the present Statute to members of a diplomatic staff may also be extended to the above-mentioned employees of the service staff, proceeding with respect to each individual state from the principle of reciprocity.

Household employees of employees of the representation, if they are not Soviet citizens or do not live in the USSR permanently, shall be exempt, on the basis of reciprocity, from taxes and assessments on wages received by them in the capacity of household employees.

Article 18.

The head of the diplomatic representation and the members of the diplomatic staff of the representation of a foreign state in a third country, traveling in transit across the territory of the USSR, shall enjoy personal inviolability and the other immunities which are necessary for ensuring their trip. This provision shall apply also to the members of their families who enjoy privileges and immunities, and who are accompanying the above-mentioned persons or traveling separately, in order to join them or to return to their country.

Diplomatic couriers traveling in transit across the territory of the USSR shall be granted the same inviolability and protection which are granted to diplomatic couriers sent to the USSR.

CONSULAR REPRESENTATIONS

Article 19.

A consular representation shall fulfill its functions within the boundaries of a consular district. The location of the consular representation and the boundaries of its consular district shall be determined by agreement between the USSR and the corresponding foreign state.

The consul general, consul, vice-consul or consular agent named by the foreign state and accepted as head of the consular representation by the Government of the USSR in the person of the Ministry of Foreign Affairs of the USSR shall be recognized as head of the consular representation.

Article 20.

The appointment of a given person as head of a consular representation shall be authenticated by a consular patent. The head of a consular representation may begin the fulfillment of his duties after issuance to him of a consular exequatur by the Ministry of Foreign Affairs of the USSR.

Article 21.

The premises occupied by a consular representation, and likewise the residence of the head of the consular representation, shall enjoy inviolability on the basis of reciprocity. Access to such premises or the conducting in them of any sort of coercive actions may take place only at the request or with the consent of the head of the consular representation or the head of the diplomatic representation of the given foreign state.

The inviolability of such premises shall not give, however, the right to use them for purposes incompatible with the functions of a consular representation.

Article 22.

The flag of the represented state may be flown, and its emblem displayed, on the premises of the consular representation.

The flag of the represented state also may be flown on the residence of the head of the consular representation and, when it is connected with the fulfillment of official duties, on his means of transportation.

Article 23.

The archives, documents and official correspondence of a consular representation shall be inviolable.

Article 24.

A consular representation may communicate without hindrance with its government, with the diplomatic representation and consular representations of its country situated on the territory of the USSR, and also with diplomatic and consular representations of its country in third states, by ordinary means of communications, by enciphered telegrams, and also by diplomatic mail. The consular representation may install radio transmitters and use them only with the permission of competent agencies of the USSR.

Article 25.

Consular officials, including the head of the consular representation, shall enjoy personal inviolability and may not be subjected to detention or arrest other than in case of prosecution for the commission of a grave crime or for the execution of a court judgment which has entered into legal forces.

They shall enjoy immunity from the criminal, civil, and administrative jurisdiction of the USSR and the union republics in all that concerns their official activity. This, however, shall not extend to suits for compensation for harm caused by road transport accidents.

Consular officials, including the head of the consular representation, and also employees of the administrative, technical and service staff of the consular representation, may not refuse to give testimony as witnesses, except for testimony on matters connected with the performance of their official duties. In the event of refusal by consular officials, including the head of the consular representation, to give testimony as witnesses, measures of compulsion may not be applied to them.

Article 26.

The consular representation shall be exempt, on the basis of reciprocity, from all general public and local taxes and assessments.

Consular officials, including the head of the consular representation, and also members of their families living together with them who are not Soviet citizens, shall be exempt, on the basis of reciprocity, from all general public and local taxes and assessments and from all personal duties.

This privilege shall also be enjoyed by employees of the administrative and technical staff of the consular representation and members of their families living with them, if such employees and the members of their families are not Soviet citizens or do not live in the USSR permanently.

Exemption from taxes and assessments shall not apply to payment for concrete types of service.

Employees of the service staff of the consular representation who are not Soviet citizens or who do not live in the USSR permanently shall enjoy, on the basis of reciprocity, exemption from taxes and assessments on wages received at their place of work, and from all personal duties. Members of their family living together with them, if they are not Soviet citizens or do not live in the USSR permanently, shall enjoy, on the basis of reciprocity, exemption from all personal duties.

Article 27.

The consular representation, consular officials, including the head of the consular representation, and the administrative and technical staff of the consular representation, and also members of their families, shall be granted, on the basis of reciprocity, the same privileges with respect to customs duties as are granted to the diplomatic representation and the corresponding personnel of the diplomatic representation.

Article 28.

On the basis of a special agreement with a foreign state, other privileges and immunities granted by the present Statute to members of a diplomatic staff may be extended to consular officials including the head of the consular representation, in addition to those provided in Articles 25-27, proceeding with respect to each individual state on the basis of reciprocity.

CONCLUDING PROVISIONS
Article 29.

The privileges and immunities provided in the present Statute for members of the diplomatic staff of a representation shall extend to representatives of foreign states, to members of parliamentary and government delegations, and also, on the basis of reciprocity, to employees of delegations of foreign states which come to the USSR to participate in international talks, international conferences and meetings, or on other official missions.

The above-mentioned persons, in traveling for the same purposes in transit across the territory of the USSR, shall enjoy personal inviolability and other immunities which are necessary for ensuring their trip.

The aforesaid shall apply members of the families of persons mentioned in this article who accompany them, if such members of the family are not Soviet citizens.

Article 30.

The privileges and immunities granted to international intergovernmental organizations on the territory of the USSR, to representatives of foreign states attached to such organizations, and also to their officials, shall be defined by the respective internatinal agreements in which the USSR participates.

Article 31.

Inclusion in the list of persons enjoying the privileges and immunities defined in the present Statute, with the exception of persons mentioned in Articles 9, 18, and 29, shall be attested by documents issued by the Ministry of Foreign Affairs of the USSR.

XIII. AGREEMENT BETWEEN THE USSR AND THE USA RELATING TO THE PROCEDURE TO BE FOLLOWED IN THE EXECUTION OF LETTERS ROGATORY, Signed November 22, 1936, 49 Stat. 3840; EAS no. 83; 167 LNTS 303.

The American Ambassador (Bullitt) to the People's Commissar for Foreign Affairs (Litvinoff)

EMBASSY OF THE UNITED STATES OF AMERICA,

Moscow, November 22 1935.

EXCELLENCY:

Confirming conversations between the American Embassy in Moscow and the People's Commissariat for Foreign Affairs with regard to the desirability of setting forth the procedure followed in our respective countries in the matter of the execution of letters rogatory issuing out of courts in the other, I have the honor to inform you of the conditions under which and the manner in which courts in the United States may execute letters rogatory issuing out of courts in the Union of Soviet Socialist Republics.

(1) Letters rogatory issuing out of courts in foreign countries are executed in the United States in accordance with the pertinent provisions of the laws of the United States, or of the State or Territory thereof in which resides the person whose testimony is desired, and in compliance with the rules of the executing court. The Government of the United States is, accordingly, not in a position to set forth with precision what may be the requirements of a particular court in the United States at a given time in respect of the execution of letters rogatory issuing out of a court in a foreign country. There are appended, however, copies of the texts of federal statutory provisions now in force which relate to the taking of testimony under commissions or letters rogatry addressed by foreign courts to federal court of the United States.

It is understood that it is the practice of American courts of appropriate jurisdiction to execute letters rogatory issuing out of foreign courts, if properly prepared and presented, anad that no difficulty is likely to be encountered by Soviet courts in obtaining the execution of letter rogatory by American courts. However, should a Soviet court encounter such difficulty, my Government would, it is understood, upon its attention being drawn thereto through the diplomatic channel, consider what steps it might appropriately take with a view to eliminating the difficulty.

(2) With respect to the question of the manner of transmittal of letters rogatory issuing out of courts in the Union of Soviet Socialist Republics and addressed to courts in the United States, I have the honor to say that neither the Department of State nor any other part of the Executive Branch of the Government of the United States makes a practice of acting as a channel for the transmittal of letters rogatory issuing out of courts in foreign countries and addressed to courts in the United States. In some States of the United States, laws have been enacted rquiring letters rogatory to be presented to the State court by the appropriate consular officer of the country in which the testimony is to be used. As my Government is of the opinion that this practice should be generally followed with respect to both Federal and State courts, letters rogatory issuing out of a court in the Soviet Union for execution in th United States should be presented to the court to which they are addressed by the consular officer of

122

the Union of Soviet Socialist Republics in the United States within whose consular district the court in question is located.

(3) While my Government is not, as has been stated above, in a position to set forth with precision what the requirements of a particular court in the United States may be at a given time in respect of the execution of letters rogatory issuing out of a court in a foreign country, my Government desires me to suggest the following points which courts in the Union of Soviet Socialist Republics may find it advantageous to observe in preparing letters rogatory for execution in the United States:

(a) The letters rogatory should be addressed by name to the court in the United States which is to execute them, if that is known; or they may be addressed "To any court of competent jurisdiction in the United States".

(b) Requests for the execution of letters rogatory should specify the name of the court out of which they issue, as well as the names of the parties to the action in which the testimony called for by the letters rogatory is desired.

(c) Requests for the execution of letters rogatory should be accompanied by English translations thereof and of accompanying documents such as exhibits and any instructions to the executing court.

With respect to the service of documents on Soviet nationals in the United States in connection with cases pending in courts in the Soviet Union, my Government has informed me that, while it cannot undertake to obligate courts or officials in the United States, no restrictions are known to exist upon the service of such documents without the application of coercion by Soviet diplomatic and consular officers in the United States.

Accept, Excellency, the renewed assurances of my highest consideration.

WILLIAM C. BULLITT

His Excellency
MAXIM M. LITVINOV,
People's Commissar for Foreign Affairs,
Moscow.

[Enclosure]

EXCERPTS FROM TITLE 28, UNITED STATES CODE.

"653. * * * When letters rogatory are addressed from any court of a foreign country to any district court of the United States, a commissioner of such district court designated by said court to make the examination of the witnesses mentioned in said letters, shall have power to compel the witnesses to appear and depose in the same manner as witnesses may be compelled to appear and testify in courts. (R. S. § 875; Feb. 27, 1887, C. 69, § 1, 19 Stat. 241)"

Testimony for use in foreign countries

"701. *Taking.* The testimony of any witness residing within the United States, to be used in any suit for the recovery of money or property depending in any court in any foreign country with which the United States are at peace, and in which the government of such foreign country shall be a party or shall have an interest, may be obtained, to be used in such suit. If a commission or letters rogatory to take such testimony, together with specific written interrogatories, accompanying the same, and addressed to such witness, shall have been issued from the court in which such suit is pending, on producing the same before the district judge of any district where the witness resides or shall be found, and on due proof being made to such judge that the testimony of any witness is material to the party desiring the same, such judge shall issue a summons to such witness requiring him to appear before the officer or commissioner named in such commission or letters rogatory, to testify in such suit. And no witness shall be compelled to appear or to testify under this section except for the purpose of answering such interrgatories so issued and accompanying such commission or letters. When counsel for all the parties attend the examination, they may consent that questions in addition to those accompanying the commission or letters rogatory may be put to the witness, unless the commission or letters rogatory exclude such additional interrogatories. The summons shall specify the time and place at which the witness is required to attend, which place shall be within one hundred miles of the place where the witness resides or shall be served with such summons. (R. S. § 4071.)

"702. *Privilege of witness.* No witness shall be required, on such examination or any other under letters rogatory, to make any disclosure or discovery which shall tend to criminate him either under the laws of the State or Territory within which such examination is had, or any other, or any foreign State. (R. S. § 4072.)

"703. *Punishment of witness for contempt.* If any person shall refuse or neglect to appear at the time and place mentioned in the summons issued, in accordance with section 701 of this title, or if upon his appearance he shall refuse to testify, he shall be liable to the same penalties as would be incurred for a like offense on the trial of a suit in the district court of the United States. (R. S. § 4073.)

"704. *Fees and mileage of witnesses.* Every witness who shall so appear and testify shall be allowed, and shall receive from the party at whose instance he shall have been summoned, the same fees and mileage as are allowed to witnesses in suits depending in the district courts of the United States. (R. S. § 4074.)"

*The People's Commissar for Foreign Affairs (Litvinoff) to the
American Ambassador (Bullitt)*

Moscow, *November "22" 1935.*

MR. AMBASSADOR:

Confirming conversations between the People's Commissariat for Foreign Affairs and the American Embassy in Moscow with regard to the desirability of setting forth the procedure followed in our respective countries in the matter of the execution of letters rogatory issuing out of the courts in the other, I have the honor to inform you of the procedure according to which the courts of the Union of Soviet Socialist Republics will accept for execution letters rogatory of courts in the United States of America.

1. Letters rogatory issuing out of courts in the United States for execution in the Union of Soviet Socialist Republics should be delivered through the diplomatic channel, i. e., through the American Embassy in Moscow and the People's Commissariat for Foreign Affairs, to the appropriate court in the Union of Soviet Socialist Republics and, when executed, they will be returned through the same channel.

2. Letters rogatory issued out of a court in the United States forwarded for execution in the Union of Soviet Socialist Republics should be addressed to the Supreme Court of that constituent republic which is competent to execute such letters rogatory. In case the exact title of the Soviet court is unknown to the court which issues the letters rogatory, the letters rogatory may be addressed "to the competent court of the Union of Soviet Socialist Republics".

3. Requests of courts in the United States for the execution of letters rogatory addressed to courts in the Union of Soviet Socialist Republics should specify the name of the court out of which they issue, as well as the names of the parties to the action in which the testimony called for by the letters rogatory is desired.

4. Requests for the execution of letters rogatory should be accompanied by Russian translations of all the basic documents, such as the interrogatories themselves and any accompanying instructions to the executing court. It will be suffient in the case of documents of secondary importance to forward short summaries of their contents in the Russian language.

5. Depending upon the nature of the letters rogatory, a fee varying from five to ten dollars ($5 to $10) will be charged for the execution of letters rogatory issued out of courts in the United States. In addition to this fee, remuneration for the services of experts as well as for the travelling expenses and expenditure of time by witnesses may be requested in individual cases, such remuneration to be based on rates current at the time fixed by law or regulation then existing. Payment of fees and other possible expenses of the nature referred to above will be effected in dollars by the American Embassy at Moscow upon receipt from the People's Commissariat for Foreign Affairs of the executed letters rogatory and an appropriate statement setting forth the amount due, and the fees and services covered thereby.

6. The court in the Union of Soviet Socialist Republics by which the letters rogatory are executed shall give effect to them in accordance with the procedural rules obtaining in the Union of Soviet Socialist Republics.

7. The court issuing the letters rogatory shall, if it so desires, be informed of the date and place where the proceedings will take place, in order that the interested parties or their legal repesentatives may, if they desire, be present.

8. The execution of letters rogatory issuing out of a court in the United States may be refused in whole or in part, if the appropriate authorities in the Union of Soviet Socialist Republics consider that the execution thereof would affect its sovereignty or safety. In returning letters rogatory unexecuted in whole or in part, the authorities refusing such execution shall affix under seal to the letters rogatory a written statement of the reasons for such refusal.

9. Any difficulties which may arise in connection with a request by a court in the United States for the execution of letters rogatory in the Union of Soviet Socialist Republics shall be settled through the diplomatic channel.

While letters rogatory must be transmitted through the diplomatic channel, American diplomatic and consular institutions may, in connection with cases pending in the United States courts, serve juridical documents on American nationals within the Union of Soviet Socialist Republics, without the application of coercion.

Accept, Mr. Ambassador, the renewed assurances of my highest consideration.

M. LITVINOFF

MR. WILLIAM C. BULLITT,
Ambassador of the United States of America,

Moscow.

XIV. CONSULAR CONVENTION BETWEEN THE GOVERNMENT OF THE UNITED STATES OF AMERICA AND THE GOVERNMENT OF THE UNION OF SOVIET SOCIALIST REPUBLICS, Signed June 1, 1964,

Department of State Bulletin, Vol. 50 (1964), p. 979.
NOTE: The Convention was signed in Moscow on June 1, 1964, but as of July 1, 1966, had not been ratified by either of the parties.

The Government of the United States of America and the Government of the Union of Soviet Socialist Republics,

Desiring to cooperate in strengthening friendly relations and to regulate consular relations between both states,

Have decided to conclude a consular convention and for this purpose have agreed on the following:

DEFINITIONS

ARTICLE 1

For the purpose of the present Convention, the terms introduced hereunder have the following meaning:

(1) "Consular establishment"—means any consulate general, consulate, vice consulate or consular agency;

(2) "Consular district"—means the area assigned to a consular establishment for the exercise of consular functions;

(3) "Head of consular establishment"—means a consul general, consul, vice consul, or consular agent directing the consular establishment;

(4) "Consular officer"—means any person, including the head of the consular establishment, entrusted with the exercise of consular functions. Also included in the definition of "consular officer" are persons assigned to the consular establishment for training in the consular service.

(5) "Employee of the consular establishment"—means any person performing administrative, technical, or service functions in a consular establishment.

OPENING OF CONSULAR ESTABISHMENTS, APPOINTMENT OF CONSULAR OFFICERS AND EMPLOYEES

ARTICLE 2

1. A consular establishment may be opened in the territory of the receiving state only with that state's consent.

2. The location of a consular establishment and the limits of its consular district will be determined by agreement between the sending and receiving states.

3. Prior to the appointment of a head of a consular establishment, the sending state shall obtain the approval of the receiving state to such an appointment through diplomatic channels.

4. The diplomatic mission of the sending state shall transmit to the foreign affairs ministry of the receiving state a consular commission which shall contain the full name of the head of the consular establishment, his citizenship, his class, the consular district assigned to him, and the seat of the consular establishment.

5. A head of a consular establishment may enter upon the exercise of his duties only after having been recognized in this capacity by the receiving state.

Such recognition after the presentation of the commission shall be in the form of a exequatur or in another form and shall be free of charge.

6. The full name, function and class of all consular officers other than the head of a consular establishment, and the full name and function of employees of the consular establishment shall be notified in advance by the sending state to the receiving state.

The receiving state shall issue to each consular officer an appropriate document confirming his right to carry out consular functions in the territory of the receiving state.

7. The receiving state may at any time, and without having to explain its decision, notify the sending state through diplomatic channels that any consular officer is persona non grata or that any employee of the consular establishment is unacceptable. In such a case the sending state shall accordingly recall such officer or employee of the consular establishment. If the sending state refuses or fails within a reasonable time to carry out its obligations under the present paragraph, the receiving state may refuse to recognize the officer or employee concerned as a member of the consular establishment.

8. With the exception of members of the staff of the diplomatic mission of the sending state, as defined in paragraph (c) of Article 1 of the Vienna Convention on Diplomatic Relations, no national of the sending state already present in the receiving state or in transit thereto may be appointed as a consular officer or employee of the consular establishment.

ARTICLE 3

Consular officers may be nationals only of the sending state.

ARTICLE 4

The receiving state shall take the necessary measures in order that a consular officer may carry out his duties and enjoy the rights, privileges, and immunities provided for in the present Convention and by the laws of the receiving state

ARTICLE 5

1. The receiving state shall either facilitate the acquisition on its territory, in accordance with its laws and regulations, by the sending state of premises necessary for its consular establishment or assist the latter in obtaining accommodation in some other way.

2. It shall also, where necessary, assist the sending state in obtaining suitable accommodation for the personnel of its consular establishment.

ARTICLE 6

1. If the head of the consular establishment cannot carry out his functions or if the position of head of a consular establishment is vacant, the sending state may empower a consular officer of the same or another consular establishment, or one of the members of the diplomatic staff of its diplomatic mission in the receiving state, to act temporarily as head of the consular establishment. The full name of this person must be transmitted in advance to the foreign affairs ministry of the receiving state.

2. A person empowered to act as temporary head of the consular establishment shall enjoy the rights, privileges and immunities of the head of the consular establishment.

3. When, in accordance with the provisions of paragraph 1 of the present Article, a member of the diplomatic staff of the diplomatic mission of the sending state in the receiving state is designated by the sending state as an acting head of the consular establishment, he shall continue to enjoy diplomatic privileges and immunities.

CONSULAR FUNCTIONS

ARTICLE 7

A consular officer shall be entitled within his consular district to perform the following functions, and for this purpose may apply orally or in writing to the competent authorities of the consular district:

(1) To protect the rights and interests of the sending state and its nationals, both individuals and bodies corporate;

(2) To further the development of commercial, economic, cultural and scientific relations between the sending state and the receiving state and otherwise promote the development of friendly relations between them;

(3) To register nationals of the sending state, to issue or amend passports and other certificates of identity, and also to issue entry, exit, and transit visas;

(4) To draw up and record certificates of birth and death of citizens of the sending state taking place in the receiving state, to record marriages and divorces, if both persons entering into marriage or divorce are citizens of the sending state, and also to receive such declarations pertaining to family relationships of a national of the sending state as may be required under the law of the sending state, unless prohibited by the laws of the receiving state;

(5) To draw up, certify, attest, authenticate, legalize and take other actions which might be necessary to validate any act or document of a legal character, as well as copies thereof, including commercial documents, declarations, registrations, testamentary dispositions, and contracts, upon the application of a national of the sending state, when such document is intended for use outside the territory of the receiving state, and also for any person, when such document is intended for use in the territory of the sending state;

(6) To translate any acts and documents into the English and Russian languages and to certify to the accuracy of the translations;

(7) To perform other official consular functions entrusted to him by the sending state if they are not contrary to the laws of the receiving state.

ARTICLE 8

1. The acts and documents specified in paragraph 5 of Article 7 of the present Convention which are drawn up or certified by the consular officer with his official seal affixed, as well as copies, extracts, and translations of such acts and documents certified by him with his official seal affixed, shall be receivable in evidence in the receiving state as official or officially certified acts, documents, copies, translations, or extracts, and shall have the same force and effect as though they were drawn up or certified by the competent authorities or officials of the receiving state; provided that such documents shall have been drawn and executed in conformity with the laws and regulations of the country where they are designed to take effect.

2. The acts, documents, copies, translations, or extracts, enumerated in paragraph 1 of the present Article shall be authenticated if required by the laws of

the receiving state when they are presented to the authorities of the receiving state when they are presented to the authorities of the receiving state.

ARTICLE 9

If the relevant information is available to the competent authorities of the receiving state, such authorities shall inform the consular establishment of the death of a national of the sending state.

ARTICLE 10

1. In the case of the death of a national of the sending state in the territory of the receiving state, without leaving in the territory of his decease any known heir or testamentary executor, the appropriate local authorities of the receiving state shall as promptly as possible inform a consular officer of the sending state.

2. A consular officer of the sending state may, within the discretion of the appropriate judicial authorities and if permissible under then existing applicable local law in the receiving state:

(a) take provisional custody of the personal property left by a deceased national of the sending state, provided that the decedent shall have left in the receiving state no heir or testamentary executor appointed by the decedent to take care of his personal estate; provided that such provisional custody shall be relinquished to a duly appointed administrator;

(b) administer the estate of a deceased national of the sending state who is not a resident of the receiving state at the time of his death, who leaves in the receiving state no heir, provided that if authorized to administer the estate, the consular officer shall relinquish such administration upon the appointment of another administrator;

(c) represent the interests of a national of the sending state in an estate in the receiving state, provided that such national is not a resident of the receiving state, unless or until such national is otherwise represented: provided, however, that nothing herein shall authorize a consular officer to act as an attorney at law.

3. Unless prohibited by law, a consular officer may, within the discretion of the court, agency, or person making distribution, receive for transmission to a national of the sending state who is not a resident of the receiving state any money or property to which such national is entitled as a consequence of the death of another person, including shares in an estate, payments made pursuant to workmen's compensation laws, pension and social benefits systems in general, and proceeds of insurance policies.

The court, agency, or person making distribution may require that a consular officer comply with conditions laid down with regard to: (a) presenting a power of attorney or other authorization from such nonresident national, (b) furnishing reasonable evidence of the receipt of such money or property by such national, and (c) returning the money or property in the event he is unable to furnish such evidence.

4. Whenever a consular officer shall perform the functions referred to in paragraphs 2 and 3 of this Article, he shall be subject, with respect to the exercise of such functions, to the laws of the receiving state and to the civil jurisdiction of the judicial and administrative authorities of the receiving state in the same manner and to the same extent as a national of the receiving state.

ARTICLE 11

A consular officer may recommend to the courts or to other competent authorities of the receiving state appropriate persons to act in the capacity of guardians or trustees for citizens of the sending state or for the property of such citizens when this property is left without supervision.

In the event that the court or competent authorities consider that the recommended candidate is for some reason unaccptable, the consular officer may propose a new candidate.

ARTICLE 12

1. A consular officer shall have the right within his district to meet with, communicate with, assist, and advise any national of the sending state and, where necessary, arrange for legal assistance for him. The receiving state shall in no way restrict the access of nationals of the sending state to its consular establishments.

2. The appropriate authorities of the receiving state shall immediately inform a consular officer of the sending state about the arrest or detention in other form of a national of the sending state.

3. A consular officer of the sending state shall have the right without delay to visit and communicate with a national of the sending state who is under arrest or otherwise detained in custody or in serving a sentence of imprisonment. The rights referred to in this paragraph shall be exercised in conformity with the laws and regulations of the receiving state, subject to the proviso, however, that the said laws and regulations must not nullify these rights.

ARTICLE 13

1. A consular officer may provide aid and assistance to vessels sailing under the flag of the sending state which have entered a port in his consular district.

2. Without prejudice to the powers of the receiving state, a consular officer may conduct investigations into any incidents which occurred during the voyage on vessels sailing under the flag of the sending state, and may settle disputes of any kind between the master, the officers and the seamen insofar as this may be authorized by the laws of the sending state. A consular officer may request the assistance of the competent authorities of the receiving state in the performance of such duties.

3. In the event that the courts or other competent authorities of the receiving state intend to take any coercive action on vessels sailing under the flag of the sending state while they are located in the waters of the receiving state, the competent authorities of the receiving state shall, unless it is impractical to do so in view of the urgency of the matter, inform a consular officer of the sending state prior to initiating such action so that the consular officer may be present when the action is taken. Whenever it is impractical to notify a consular officer in advance, the competent authorities of the receiving state shall inform him as soon as possible thereafter of the action taken.

4. Paragraph 3 of this Article shall not apply to customs, passport, and sanitary inspections, or to action taken at the request or with the approval of the master of the vessel.

5. The term "vessel", as used in the present Convention, does not include warships.

ARTICLE 14

If a vessel sailing under the flag of the sending state suffers shipwreck, runs aground, is swept ashore, or suffers any other accident whatever within the territorial limits of the receiving state, the competent authorities of the receiving state shall immediately inform a consular officr and advise him of the measures which they haev taken to rescue persons, vessel, and cargo.

The consular officer may provide all kinds of assistance to such a vessel, the members of its crew, and its pasengers, as well as take measures in connection with the preservation of the cargo and repair of the ship, or he may request the authorities of the receiving state to take such measures.

The competent authorities of the receiving state shall render the necessary assistance to the consular officer in measures taken by him in connection with the accident to the vessel.

No customs duties shall be levied against a wrecked vessel, its cargo or stores, state.

If the owner or anyone authorized to act for him is unable to make necessary arrangements in connection with the vessel or its cargo, the consular officer may make such arrangements. The consular officer may under similar circumstances make arrangements in connection with cargo owned by the sending state or any of its nationals and found or brought into port from a wrecked vessel sailing under the flag of any state except a vessel of the receiving state.

ARTICLE 15

Articles 13 and 14, respectively, shall also apply to aircraft.

RIGHTS, PRIVILEGES AND IMMUNITIES

ARTICLE 16

The national flag of the sending state and the consular flag may be flown at the consular establishment, at the residence of the head of the consular establishment, and on his means of transport used by him in the performance of his official duties. The shield with the national coat-of-arms of the sending state and the name of the establishment may also affixed on the building in which the consular establishment is located.

ARTICLE 17

The consular archives shall be inviolable at all times and wherever they may be. Unofficial papers shall not be kept in the consular archives.

The buildings or parts of buildings and the land ancillary thereto, used for the purposes of the consular establishment and the residence of the head of the consular establishment, shall be inviolable.

The police and other authorities of the receiving state may not enter the building establishment or the residence of the head of the consular establishment without the consent of the head thereof, persons appointed by him, or the head of the diplomatic mission of the sending state.

ARTICLE 18

1. The consular establishment shall have the right to communicate with its Government, with the diplomatic mission and the consular establishments of the

sending state in the receiving state, or with other diplomatic missions and consular establishments of the sending state, making use of all ordinary means of communication. In such communications, the consular establishment shall have the right to use code, diplomatic couriers, and the diplomatic pouch. The same fees shall apply to consular establishments in the use of ordinary means of communication as apply to the diplomatic mission of the sending state.

2. The official correspondence of a consular establishment, regardless of what means of communication are used, and the sealed diplomatic pouch bearing visible external marks of its official character, shall be inviolable and not subject to examination or detention by the authorities of the receiving state.

ARTICLE 19

1. Consular officers shall not be subject to the jurisdiction of the receiving state in matters relating to their official activity. The same applies to employees of the consular establishment, if they are nationals of the sending state.

2. Consular officers and employees of the consular establishment who are nationals of the sending state shall enjoy immunity from the criminal jurisdiction of the receiving state.

3. This immunity from the criminal jurisdiction of the receiving state of consular officers and employees of the consular establishment of the sending state may be waived by the sending state. Waiver must always be express.

ARTICLE 20

1. Consular officers and employees of the consular establishment, on the invitation of a court of the receiving state, shall appear in court for witness testimony. Taking measures to compel a consular officer or an employee of the consular establishment who is a national of the sending state to appear in court as a witness and to give witness testimony is not permissible.

2. If a consular officer or an employee of the consular establishment who is a national of the sending state for official reasons or for reasons considered valid according to the laws of the receiving state cannot appear in court, he shall inform the court thereof and give witness testimony on the premises of the consular establishment or in his own abode.

3. Whenever under the laws of the receiving state an oath is required to be taken in court by consular officers and employees of the consular establishment, an affirmation shall be accepted in lieu thereof.

4. Consular officers and employees of the consular establishment may refuse to give witness testimony on facts relating to their official activity.

5. The provisions of paragraphs 1, 2, 3, and 4 shall also apply to proceedings conducted by administrative authorities.

ARTICLE 21

1. Immovable property, situated in the territory of the receiving state, of which the sending state or one or more persons acting in its behalf is the owner or lessee and which is used for diplomatic or consular purposes, including residences for personnel attached to the diplomatic and consular establishments, shall be exempt from taxation of any kind imposed by the receiving state or any of its states or local governments other than such as represent payments for specific services rendered.

2. The exemption from taxation referred to in paragraph 1 of this Article shall not apply to such charges, duties, and taxes if, under the law of the receiving

state, they are payable by the person who contracted with the sending state or with the person acting on its behalf.

ARTICLE 22

A consular officer or employee of a consular establishment, who is not a national of the receiving state and who does not have the status in the receiving state of an alien lawfully admitted for permanent residence, shall be exempt from the state or any of its states or local governments on official emoluments, salaries, wages, or allowances received by such officer or employee from the sending state in connection with the discharge of his official functions.

ARTICLE 23

1. A consular officer or employee of a consular establishment who is not a national of the receiving state and who does not have the status in the receiving state of an alien lawfully admitted for permanent residence, shall, except as provided in paragraph 2 of this Article, be exempt from the payment of all taxes or similar charges of any kind imposed by the receiving state or any of its states or local governments, for the payment of which the officer or employee of the consular establishment would otherwise be legally liable.

2. The exemption from taxes or charges provided in paragraph 1 of this Article does not apply in respect to taxes or charges upon:

(a) The acquisition or possession of private immovable property located in the receiving state if the persons referred to in paragraph 1 of this Article do not own or lease this property on the behalf of the sending state for the purposes of the consular establishment;

(b) Income received from sources in the receiving state other than as described in Article 22 of the present Convention;

(c) The transfer by gift of property in the receiving state;

(d) The transfer at death, including by inheritance, of property in the receiving state.

3. However, the exemption from taxes or similar charges provided in paragraph 1 of this Article, applies in respect to movable inherited property left after the death of a consular officer or employee of the consular establishment or a member of his family residing with him if they are not nationals of the receiving state or aliens lawfully admitted for permanent residence, and if the property was located in the receiving state exclusively in connection with the sojourn in this state of the deceased as a consular officer or employee of the consular establishment or member of his family residing with him.

ARTICLE 24

A consular officr or employee of a consular establishment and members of his family residing with him who are not nationals of the receiving state and who do not have the status in the receiving state of aliens lawfully admitted for permanent residence, shall be exempt in the receiving state from service in the armed forces and from all other types of compulsory service.

ARTICLE 25

his family residing with him who do not have the status in the receiving state of aliens lawfully admitted for permanent residence, shall be exempt from all

134

obligations under the laws and regulations of the receiving state with regard to the registration of aliens, and obtaining permission to reside, and from compliance with other similar requirements applicable to aliens.

ARTICLE 26

1. The same full exemption from customs duties and internal revenue or other taxes imposed upon or by reason of importation shall apply in the receiving state to all articles, including motor vehicles, imported exclusively for the official use of a consular establishment, as applies to articles imported for the official use of the diplomatic mission of the sending state.

2. Consular officers, and employees of the consular establishment, and members of their families residing with them, who are not nationals of the receiving state, and who do not have the status in the receiving state of aliens lawfully admitted for permanent residence, shall be granted, on the basis of reciprocity, the same exemptions from customs duties and internal revnue or other taxes imposed upon or by reason of importation, as are granted to corresponding personnel of the diplomatic mission of the sending state.

3. For the purpose of paragraph 2 of this Article the term "corresponding personnel of the diplomatic mission" refers to members of the diplomatic staff in the case of consular officers, and to members of the administrative and technical staff in the case of employees of a consular establishment.

ARTICLE 27

Subject to the laws and regulations of the receiving state concerning zones entry into which is prohibited or regulated for reasons of national security, a consular officer shall be permitted to travel freely within the limits of his consular district to carry out his official duties.

ARTICLE 28

Without prejudice to their privileges and immunities, it is the duty of all persons enjoying such privileges and immunities to respect the laws and regulations of the receiving state, including traffic regulations.

ARTICLE 29

1. The rights and obligations of consular officers provided for in the present Convention also apply to members of the diplomatic staff of the diplomatic mission of the Contracting Parties charged with the performance of consular functions in the diplomatic mission and who have been notified in a consular capacity to the foreign affairs ministry of the receiving state by the diplomatic mission.

2. Except as provided in paragraph 4 of Article 10 of the present Convention, the performance of consular functions by the persons referred to in paragraph 1 of this Article shall not affect the diplomatic privileges and immunities granted to them as members of the diplomatic mission.

FINAL PROVISIONS

ARTICLE 30

1. The present Convention shall be subject to ratification and shall enter into force on the thirtieth day following the exchange of instruments of ratification, which shall take place in Washington as soon as possible.

2. The Convention shall remain in force until six months from the date on which one of the Contracting Parties informs the other Contracting Party of its desire to terminate its validity.

In witness whereof the Plenipotentiaries of the two Contracting Parties have signed the present Convention and affixed their seals thereto.

Done in Moscow on June 1, 1964 in two copies, each in the English and the Russian language, both texts being equally authentic.

For the Government of the United States of America:

FOY D. KOHLER
Ambassador of the United States of America to the U.S.S.R.

For the Government of the Union of Soviet Socialist Republics:

A. GROMYKO
Minister for Foreign Affairs of the Union of Soviet Socialist Republics

Protocol to the Consular Convention Between the Government of the
United States of America and the Government of the Union of
Soviet Socialist Republics

1. It is agreed between the Contracting Parties that the notification of a consular officer of the arrest or detention in other form of a national of the sending state specified in paragraph 2 of Article 12 of the Consular Convention between the Government of the United States of America and the Government of the Union of Soviet Socialist Republics of June 1, 1964, shall take place within one to three days from the time of arrest or detention depending on conditions of communication.

2. It is agreed between the Contracting Parties that the rights specifiied in paragraph 3 of Article 12 of the Consular Convention of a consular officer to visit and communicate with a national of the sending state who is under arrest or otherwise detained in custody shall be accorded within two to four days of the arrest or detention of such national depending upon his location.

3. It is agreed between the Contracting Parties that the rights specified in paragraph 3 of Article 12 of the Consular Convention of a consular officer to visit and communicate with a national of the sending state who is under arrest or otherwise detained in custody or is serving a sentence of imprisonment shall be accorded on a continuing basis.

The present Protocol constitutes an integral part of the Consular Convention between the Government of the United States of America and the Government of the Union of Soviet Socialist Republics of June 1, 1964.

Done at Moscow on June 1, 1964 in two copies, each in the English and the Russian language, both texts being equally authentic.

For the Government of the United States of America:

FOY D. KOHLER
Ambassador of the United States of America to the U.S.S.R.

For the Government of the Union of Soviet Socialist Republics:

A. GROMYKO
Minister for Foreign Affairs of the Union of Soviet Socialist Republics

XV. CONVENTION ON THE LEGAL CAPACITY, PRIVILEGES, AND IMMUNITIES OF THE COUNCIL FOR MUTUAL ECONOMIC ASSISTANCE, Signed December 14, 1959, *Vedomosti,* 1960, no. 15, item 108.

The governments of the People's Republic of Albania, the People's Republic of Bulgaria, the Hungarian People's Republic, the German Democratic Republic, the Polish People's Republic, the Rumanian People's Republic, the Union of Soviet Socialist Republics, and the Czechoslovak Republic, taking into consideration Article XIII of the Charter of the Council for Mutual Economic Assistance, which provides:

that the Council shall enjoy on the territory of each member country of the Council the legal capacity necessary for fulfilling its functions and achieving its purposes;

that the Council, and also the representatives of the member countries of the of these countries the privileges and immunities necessary for fulfilling its functions and achieving the purposes provided in the above-mentioned Charter;

and that the said legal capacity, privileges, and immunities shall be defined in a special Convention, have agreed to the following:

Article I

Legal Capacity

The Council for Mutual Economic Assistance shall be a juridical person and shall be empowered:

(a) to conclude agreements;

(b) to acquire, rent and dispose of property;

(c) to appear in court.

Article II

Property, Assets, Documents

1. The premises of the Council for Mutual Economic Assistance shall be inviolable. Its property, assets and documents, wherever located, shall enjoy immunity from any form of administrative or judicial interference, except when the Council itself waives immunity in a particular instance.

2. The Council for Mutual Economic Assistance shall be exempt from all direct taxes and assessments, both statewide and local. This provision shall not be applied with respect to payments for the supplying of municipal and other similar services.

3. The Council for Mutual Economic Assistance shall be exempt from customs duties and from limitations on the import and export of items intended for official use.

Article III

Communications Privileges

The Council for Mutual Economic Assistance shall enjoy on the territory of each of the member countries of the Council conditions with respect to priority, tariffs, and rates for postal, telegraph, and telephone communications no less favorable than those enjoyed by diplomatic representations in the respective country.

Article IV

Representatives of Member Countries of the Council

1. In the performance of their official duties in the agencies of the Council, and also at meetings conducted within the framework of the Council, the representatives of the member countries of the Council for Mutual Economic Assistance shall be granted the following privileges and immunities on the territory of each member country of the Council:

(a) immunity from personal arrest or detention, and also from the jurisdiction of judicial institutions with respect to all actions which may be performed by them in the capacity of representative;

(b) inviolability of all papers and documents;

(c) the same customs privileges with respect to their personal baggage as are granted to personnel of equivalent rank of diplomatic representations in the given country;

(d) exemption from personal obligations and from direct taxes and assessments with respect to wages paid them by the country that appointed them.

2. The representatives of the countries in the Council and their deputies shall enjoy, in addition to the privileges and immunities indicated in paragraph 1 of the present article, privileges and immunities granted in the given country to diplomatic representatives .

3. The privileges and immunities provided by the present Article shall be granted to the persons mentioned in it exclusively for official purposes. Each member country of the Council shall have the right and shall be obliged to waive the immunity of its representative in all cases in which, in the opinion of such country, the immunity would interfere with the administration of justice and a waiver of immunity would not cause injury to the purposes in connection with which it was granted.

4. The provisions of Paragraphs 1 and 2 of this Article shall not be applied to relations between representatives and the agencies of the country of which he is a citizen.

5. The definition of "representative" in the present Article shall include the representatives of countries in the Council, their deputies, the heads, members and secretaries of delegations and also advisors and experts.

Article V

Officials of the Council

1. The Consultative Body of Representatives of the countries of the Council for Mutual Economic Assistance, on the proposal of the Secretary of the Council, shall define the categories of officials to whom the provisions of the present Article shall be applied. The names of such officials shall be periodically communicated by the Secretary of the Council to the competent agencies of the member countries of the Council.

2. On the territory of each member country of the Council, the officials of the Council:

(a) shall not be subject to judicial or administrative responsibility for acts which may be performed by them in the capacity of officials;

(b) shall be exempt from personal duties;

(c) shall be exempt from direct taxes and assessments with respect to wages paid them by the Council;

138

(d) shall have the right to the same customs privileges with respect to their personal baggage as are granted to personnel of equivalent rank of diplomatic representations in the given country.

3. The Secretary of the Council and his deputies shall enjoy, in addition to the privileges and immunities provided in Paragraph 2 of the present Article, the privileges and immunities granted in the given country to diplomatic representatives.

4. The privileges and immunities stipulated by the present Article shall be granted to the persons mentioned in it exclusively in the interests of the Council and independently of the exercise by those officials of their official functions. The Secretary of the Council shall have the right, and shall be obliged, to waive the immunity granted to any official in those instances when, in his opinion, the immunity would interfere with the administration of justice and immunity may be waived without injury to the interest of the Council. With respect to the Secretary of the Council and his deputies, the right to waive immunity shall belong to the Consultative Body of Representatives of the countries of the Council.

3. The provisions of Paragraphs 2 (b) and (c) of the present Article shall, not apply to officials of the Council who are citizens of the country where the agency of the Council in which they work is located.

Article VI

Concluding Declarations

[Formal provisions concerning signature, ratification and entry into force. Text omitted]

XVI. CONVENTION ON THE PRIVILEGES AND IMMUNITIES OF THE UNITED NATIONS, Adopted by the General Assembly of the United Nations on February 13, 1946, United Nations Treaty Series, I, p. 15.

NOTE: The USSR deposited an act of accession to the Convention on September 22, 1953. (As of June 1, 1966, the United States had not acceded to the Convention). The Soviet act of accession contained the following reservation, to which the Government of the United Kingdom has objected:

The Soviet Union does not consider itself bound by the provision of section 30 of the Convention which envisages the compulsory jurisdiction of the International Court and, in regard to the competence of the International Court in differences arising out of the interpretation and application of the Convention, the Soviet Union will, as hitherto, adhere to the position that, for the submission of a particular dispute for settlement by the International Court, the consent of all, the parties to the dispute is required in every individual case. This reservation is equally applicable to the provisions contained in the same section, whereby the advisory opinion of the International Court shall be accepted as decisive.

Whereas Article 104 of the Charter of the United Nations provides that the Organization shall enjoy in the territory of each of its Members such legal capacity as may be necessary for the exercise of its functions and the fulfilment of its purposes and

Whereas Article 105 of the Charter of the United Nations provides that the Organization shall enjoy in the territory of each of its Members such privileges and immunities as are necessary for the fulfilment of its purposes and that representatives of the Members of the United Nations and officials of the Organization shall similarly enjoy such privileges and immunities as are necessary for the independent exercise of their functions in connection with the Organization.

Consequently the General Assembly by a Resolution adopted on the 13 February 1946, approved the following Convention and proposed it for accession by each Member of the United Nations.

Article I

SECTION 1. The United Nations shall possess juridical personality. It shall have the capacity:

    (a) To contract;
    (b) To acquire and dispose of immovable and movable property;
    (c) To institute legal proceedings.

Article II

PROPERTY, FUNDS AND ASSETS

SECTION 2. The United Nations, its property and assets wherever located and by whomsoever held, shall enjoy immunity from every form of legal process except insofar as in any particular case it has expressly waived its immunity shall extend to any particular case it has expressly waived it immunity [*sic*]. It is, however, understood that no waiver of immunity shall extend to any measure of execution.

140

SECTION 3. The premises of the United Nations shall be inviolable. The property and assets of the United Nations, wherever located and by whomsoever held, shall be immune from search, requisition, confiscation, expropriation and any other form of interference, whether by executive, administrative, judicial or legislative action.

SECTION 4. The archives of the United Nations, and in general all documents belonging to it or held by it, shall be inviolable wherever located.

SECTION 5. Without being restricted by financial controls, regulations or moratoria of any kind,

(a) The United Nations may hold funds, gold or currency of any kind and operate accounts in any currency;

(b) The United Nations shall be free to transfer its funds, gold or currency from one country to another or within any country and to convert any currency held by it into any other currency.

SECTION 6. In exercising its rights under Section 5 above, the United Nations shall pay due regard to any representations made by the Government of any Member insofar as it is considered that effect can be given to such representations without detriment to the interests of the United Nations.

SECTION 7. The United Nations, its assets, income and other property shall be:

(a) Exempt from all direct taxes; it is understood, however, that the United Nations will not claim exemption from taxes which are, in fact, no more than charges for public utility services;

(b) Exempt from customs duties and prohibitions and restrictions on imports and exports in respect of articles imported or exported by the United Nations for its official use. It is understood, however, that articles imported under such exemption will not be sold in the country into which they were imported except under conditions agreed with the Government of that country;

(c) Exempt from customs duties and prohibitions and restrictions on imports and exports in respect of its publications.

SECTION 8. While the United Nations will not, as a general rule, claim exemption from excise duties and from taxes on the sale of movable and immovable property which form part of the price to be paid, nevertheless when the United Nations is making important purchases for official use of property on which such duties and taxes have been charged or are chargeable, Members will, whenever possible, make appropriate administrative arrangements for the remission or return of the amount of duty or tax.

Article III

FACILITIES IN RESPECT OF COMMUNICATIONS

SECTION 9. The United Nations shall enjoy in the territory of each Member for its official communications treatment not less favourable than that accorded by the Government of that Member to any other Government including its diplomatic mission in the matter of priorities, rates and taxes on mails, cables, telegrams, radiograms, telephotos, telephone and other communications; and press rates for information to the press and radio. No censorship shall be applied to the official correspondence and other official communications of the United Nations.

SECTION 10. The United Nations shall have the right to use codes and to despatch and receive its correspondence by courier or in bags, which shall have the same immunities and privileges as diplomatic couriers and bags.

Article IV

THE REPRESENTATIVES OF MEMBERS

SECTION 11. Representatives of Members to the principal and subsidiary organs of the United Nations and to conferences convened by the United Nations, shall, while exercising their functions and during the journey to and from the place of meeting, enjoy the following privileges and immunities:

(a) Immunity from personal arrest or detention and from seizure of their personal baggage, and, in respect of words spoken or written and all acts done by them in their capacity as representatives, immunity from legal process of every kind;

(a) [sic] Inviolability for all papers and documents;

(c) The right to use codes and receive papers or correspondence by courier or in sealed bags;

(d) Exemption in respect of themselves and their spouses from immigration restrictions, aliens registration or national service obligations in the state they are visiting or through which they are passing in the exercise of their functions;

(e) The same facilities in respect of currency or exchange restrictions as are accorded to representatives of foreign governments on temporary official missions;

(f) The same immunities and facilities in respect of their personal baggage as are accorded to diplomatic envoys, and also;

(g) Such other privileges, immunities and facilities not inconsistent with the foregoing as diplomatic envoys enjoy, except that they shall have no right to claim exemption from customs duties on goods imported (otherwise than as part of their personal baggage) or from excise duties or sales taxes.

SECTION 12. In order to secure, for the representatives of Members to the principal and subsidiary organs of the United Nations and to conferences convened by the United Nations, complete freedom of speech and independence [sic] in the discharge of their duties, the immunity from legal process in respect of words spoken or written and all acts done by them in discharging their duties shall continue to be accorded, notwithstanding that the persons concerned are no longer the representatives of Members.

SECTION 13. Where the incidence of any form of taxation depends upon residence, periods during which the representatives of Members to the principal and subsidiary organs of the United Nations and to conferences convened by of the United Nations and not for the personal benefit of the individuals themnot be considered as periods of residence.

SECTION 14 Privileges and immunities are accorded to the representatives of Members not for the personal benefit of the individuals themselves, but in order to safeguard the independent exercise of their functions in connection with the United Nations. Consequently a Member not only has the right but is under a duty to waive the immunity of its representative in any case where in the opinion of the Member the immunity would impede the course of justice, and it can be waived without prejudice to the purpose for which the immunity is accorded.

SECTION 15. The provisions of Sections 11, 12 and 13 are not applicable as between a representative and the authorities of the state of which he is a national or of which he is or has been the representative.

142

SECTION 16. In this article the expression "representatives" shall be deemed to include all delegates, advisers, technical experts and secretaries of delegations.

Article V

OFFICIALS

SECTION 17. The Secretary-General will specify the categories of officials to which the provisions of this Article and Article VII shall apply. He shall submit these categories to the General Assembly. Thereafter these categories shall be communicated to the Governments of all Members. The names of the officials included in these categories shall from time to time be made known to the Governments of Members.

SECTION 18. Officials of the United Nations shall:

(*a*) Be immune from legal process in respect of words spoken or written and all acts performed by them in their official capacity;

(*b*) Be exempt from taxation on the salaries and emoluments paid to them by the United Nations;

(*c*) Be immune from national service obligations;

(*d*) Be immune, together with their spouses and relatives dependent on them, from immigration restrictions and alien registration;

(*e*) Be accorded the same privileges in respect of exchange facilities as are accorded to the officials of comparable ranks forming part of diplomatic missions to the Government concerned;

(*f*) Be given, together with their spouses and relatives dependent on them, the same repatriation facilities in time of international crisis as diplomatic envoys;

(*g*) Have the right to import free of duty their furniture and effects at the time of first taking up their post in the country in question.

SECTION 19. In addition to the immunities and privileges specified in Section 18, the Secretary-General and all Assistant Secretaries-General shall be accorded in respect of themselves, their spouses and minor children, the privileges and immunities, exemptions and facilities accorded to diplomatic envoys, in accordance with international law.

SECTION 20. Privileges and immunities are granted to officials in the interests of the United Nations and not for the personal benefit of th individuals themselves. The Secretary-General shall have the right and the duty to waive the immunity of any official in any case where, in his opinion, the immunity would impede the course of justice and can be waived without prejudice to the interests of the United Nations. In the case of the Secretary-General, the Security Council shall have the right to waive immunity.

SECTION 21. The United Nations shall co-operate at all times with the appropriate authorities of Members to facilitate the proper administration of justice, secure the observance of police regulations and prevent the occurence of any abuse in connection with the privileges, immunities and facilities mentioned in this Article.

Article VI

EXPERTS ON MISSIONS FOR THE UNITED NATIONS

SECTION 22. Experts (other than officials coming within the scope of Article V) performing missions for the United Nations shall be accorded such privileges and immunities as are necessary for the independent exercise of their functions during the period of their missions, including the time spent on journeys in connection with their missions. In particular they shall be accorded:

(*a*) Immunity from personal arrest or detention and from seizure of their personal baggage;

(*b*) In respect of words spoken or written and acts done by them in the course of the performance of their mission, immunity from legal process of every kind. This immunity from legal process shall continue to be accorded notwithstanding that the persons concerned are no longer employed on missions for the United Nations;

(*c*) Inviolability for all papers and documents;

(*d*) For the purpose of their communications with the United Nations, the right to use codes and to receive papers or correspondence by courier or in sealed bags;

(*e*) The Same facilities in respect of currency or exchange restrictions as are accorded to representatives of foreign governments on temporary official missions;

(*f*) The same immunities and facilities in respect of their personal baggage as are accorded to diplomatic envoys.

SECTION 23. Privileges and immunities are granted to experts in the interests of the United Nations and not for the personal benefit of the individuals themselves. The Secretary-General shall have the right and the duty to waive the immunity of any expert in any cases where, in his opinion, the immunity would impede the course of justice and it can be waived without prejudice to the interests of the United Nations.

Article VIII

UNITED NATIONS LAISSEZ-PASSER

SECTION 24. The United Nations may issue United Nations laissez-passer to its officials. These laissez-passer shall be recognized and accepted as valid travel documents by the authorities of Members, taking into account the provisions of Section 25.

SECTION 25. Applications for visas (where required) from the holders of United Nations laissez-passer, when accompanied by a certificate that they are travelling on the business of the United Nations, shall be dealt with as speedily as possible. In addition, such persons shall be granted facilities for speedy travel.

SECTION 26. Similar facilities to those specified in Section 25 shall be accorded to experts and other persons who, though not the holders of United Nations laissez-passer, have a certificate that they are travelling on the business of the United Nations.

SECTION 27. The Secretary-General, Assistant Secretaries-General and Directors travelling on United Nations laissez-passer on the business of the United Nations shall be granted the same facilities as are accorded to diplomatic envoys.

SECTION 28. The provisions of this article may be applied to the comparable officials of specialized agencies if the agreements for relationship made under Article 63 of the Charter so provide.

Article VIII

SETTLEMENTS OF DISPUTES

SECTION 29. The United Nations shall make provisions for appropriate modes of settlement of:

(a) Disputes arising out of contracts or other disputes of a private law character to which the United Nations is a party;

(b) Disputes involving any officials of the United Nations who by reason of his official position enjoys immunity, if immunity has not been waived by the Secretary-General.

SECTION 30. All differences arising out of the interpretation or application of the present convention shall be referred to the International Court of Justice, unless in any case it is agreed by the parties to have recourse to another mode of settlement. If a difference arises between the United Nations on the one hand and a Member on the other hand, a request shall be made for an advisory opinion on any legal question involved in accordance with Article 96 of the Charter and Article 65 of the Statute of the Court. The opinion given by the Court shall be accepted as decisive by the parties.

Final Article

SECTION 31. This convention is submitted to every member of the United Nations for accession.

SECTION 32. Accession shall be affected by deposit of an instrument with the Secretary-General of the United Nations and the convention shall come into force as regards each Member on the date of deposit of each instrument of accession.

SECTION 33. The Secretary-General shall inform all Members of the United Nations of the deposit of each accession.

SECTION 34. It is understood that, when an instrument of accession is deposited on behalf of any Member, the Member will be in a position under its own law to give effect to the terms of this convention.

SECTION 35. This convention shall continue in force as between the United Nations and every Member which has deposited an instrument of accession for so long as that Member remains a Member of the United Nations, or until a revised general convention has been approved by the General Assembly and that Member has become a party to this revised convention.

SECTION 36. The Secretary-General may conclude with any Member or Members supplementary agreements adjusting the provisions of this convention so far as that Member or those Members are concerned. These supplementary agreements shall in each case be subject to the approval of the General Assembly.

BIBLIOGRAPHY

Introductory Note

This bibliography is in two parts. The first lists works cited in the text. The second suggests sources, mainly in the English language, for readers who wish to become further acquainted with Soviet domestic and international legal practice.

PART I: WORKS CITED IN THE TEXT

1. Books and Monographs

Berezovskaia, S. G., *Okhrana prav grazhdan Sovetskoi prokuraturoi* [Protection of the Rights of Citizens by the Soviet Procuracy] (Moscow, 1964).

Berman, Harold J., *Soviet Criminal Law and Procedure: The RSFSR Codes* (Cambridge, Mass., 1966) Translation by Harold J. Berman and James W. Spindler.

Berman, Harold J., *Justice in the USSR: An Interpretation of Soviet Law* (2nd ed., rev. and enl., Cambridge, Mass., 1963).

Bishop, Donald G., *The Roosevetl-Litvinov Agreements* (Syracuse, 1965).

Blishchenko, I. P. and V. N. Durkenevskii, *Diplomaticheskoe i konsul'skoe pravo* [Diplomatic and Consular Law] (Moscow, 1962).

Boguslavskii, M. M. and A. A. Rubanov, *Pravovoe polozhenie inostrantsev v SSSR* [The Legal Status of Foreigners in the USSR] (Moscow, 1959); (2nd ed., revised and enlarged, Moscow, 1962); English language edition under the title *The Legal Status of Foreigners in the USSR* (Moscow, 1960?). The text of each of the three editions is slightly different. The 1962 Russian edition gives the most up-to-date and realistic picture of the status of aliens in the USSR, although it does not discuss the harassment of aliens that sometimes takes place in practice, either within existing law or in violation of it. It contains a bibliography of Soviet legislation dealing with the rights of foreigners.

Boldyrev, V. A., general editor, *Nauchno-prakticheskii kommentarii k ugolonomu protsessual'nomu kodeksu RSFSR* [A Scholarly and Practical Commentary to the Criminal Procedure Code of the RSFSR] (Moscow, 1963).

Bratus', S. N. and E. A. Fleishits, editors, *Nauchno-prakticheskii kommentarii k osnovam grazhdanskogo zakonodatel'stva Soiuza SSR i Soiuznykh Respublik* [A Scholarly and Practical Commentary to the Fundamental Principles of Civil Legislation of the USSR and the Union Republics] (Moscow, 1962).

Braude, L. L. *Vozmeshchenie ushcherba pri iz"iatii zemli* [Compensation for Loss in Land Taking] (Moscow, 1960).

Chernov, V. and V. Mazov, *Moscow, A Tourist's Guide* (2nd ed., Moscow, 1962).

Cooper, Dennis A., *The Air Code of the USSR* (Charlottesville, Va., 1966).

Davydov, G. P. and V. I. Mazurenko, *Prepodavanie Konstitutsii SSR v shkole* [Teaching the Constitution of the USSR in School] (D. S. Karev, ed., 2nd enl. ed., Moscow, 1961).

Denisov, A. and M. Kirichenko, *Soviet State Law* (Moscow, 1960).

De Witt, Nicholas, *Education and Professional Employment in the USSR* (Washington, 1961).

Genkin, D. M., general editor, *Pravovoe regulirovanie vneshnei torgovli SSSR* [The Legal Regulation of the Foreign Trade of the USSR] (Moscow, 1961).

Gornyi, A. G., editor, *Nauchno-prakticheskii kommentarii k zakonu ob ugolovnoi otvet-stvennosti za voinskie prestupleniia* [A Scholarly and Practical Commentary to the Law on Criminal Liability for Military Crimes] (2nd ed., Moscow, 1961).

Gsovski, Vladimir, *Soviet Civil Law* (2 vols., Ann Arbor, 1948-1949).

Hazard, John N. and Isaac Shapiro, *The Soviet Legal System, Post-Stalin Documentation and Historical Commentary* (New York, 1962). An extensive collection of translated excerpts from recent Soviet legislation, judicial decisions, books, and articles. Also contains brief historical commentaries and excellent bibliographies.

Henkin, Louis, *Arms Control and Inspection in American Law* (New York, 1958).

Kozlov, Iu. M., editor, *Sovetskoe administrativnoe pravo (obshchaia chast')* [Soviet Administrative Law (General Part)] (Moscow, 1962).

Kozlov, Iu. M., editor, *Sovetskoe administrativnoe pravo (osobennaia chast')* [Soviet Administrative Law (Special Part)] (Moscow, 1964).

Lauterpacht, H., editor, L. Oppenheim, *International Law*, Vol. I, *Peace* (8th ed., New York, 1955).

Lepeshkin, A. I., *Kurs sovetskogo gosudarstvennogo prava* [Textbook of Soviet State Law], Vol. I (Moscow, 1961); Vol. II (Moscow, 1962).

Lunev, A. E., *Obespechenie zakonnosti v sovetskom gosudarstvennom upravlenii* [Guaranteeing Legality in Soviet State Administration] (Moscow, 1963).

Lunts, L. A., *Mezhdunarodnoe chastnoe pravo, osobennaia chast'* [Private International Law, Special Part] (Moscow, 1963).

Men'shagin, V. D., and B. A. Kurinov, *Nauchno-prakticheskii kommentarii k osnovam ugolovnogo zakonodatel'stva Soiuza SSR i soiuznkyh respublik* [A Scholarly and Practical Commentary to the Fundamental Principles of Criminal Legislation of the USSR and the Union Republics] (2nd ed., Moscow, 1961).

Morgan, Glenn G., *Soviet Administrative Legality: The Role of the Attorney General's Office* (Stanford, 1962).

Nikiforov, B. S., general editor, *Nauchno-prakticheskii kommentarii k ugolovnomu kodeksu RSFSR* [A Scholarly and Practical Commentary to the Criminal Code of the RSFSR] (2nd ed., Moscow, 1964).

Shurshalov, V. M., general editor, *Mezhdunarondo-pravovye formy sotrudnichestvo sotsialisticheskikh gosudarstv* [International Law Forms of Collaboration of Socialist States] Moscow, 1962.

Studenikin, S. S., general editor, *Istoriia sovetskoi Konstitutsii (v dokumentakh), 1917-1956* [A History of the Soviet Constitution (in Documents), 1917-1956] (Moscow, 1957).

Triska, Jan. F., and Robert M. Slusser, *The Theory, Law and Policy of Soviet Treaties* (Stanford, 1962).

United States Senate, Committee on Government Operation, Staffing Procedure and Problems in the Soviet Union (Washington, 1963).

Vlasov, V. A. and S. S. Studenikin, *Sovetskoe administrativnoe pravo* [Soviet Administrative Law] (Moscow, 1959).

Zdir, Ia. A. *Gosudarstvennye inspektsii v SSSR* [State Inspection Agencies in the USSR] (Moscow, 1960).

2. Articles

Fisher, Roger, "Internal Enforcement of International Rules" in Seymour Melman, editor, *Disarmament: Its Policies and Economics* (Boston 1962), p. 9.

Ginsburgs, George and Armins Rusis, "Soviet Criminal Law and the Protection of State Secrets" in University of Leyden *Law in Eastern Europe*, no. 7 (Leyden, 1963), pp. 3-48.

Gray, Whitmore, "Soviet Tort Law: The New Principles Annotated" *University of Illinois Law Forum*, vol. 1964, no. 1, p. 180.

Loeber, Dietrich A. "The Soviet Procuracy and the Rights of the Individual Against the State" *Journal of the International Commission of Jurists*, vol. I (1957), pp. 59-105.

Maggs, Peter, "Der nichtmilitärischer Geheimschutz nach Sowjetrecht," *Osteuropa-Recht*, Vol. 11 (1965), p. 161.

Mikhailov, M. *"Nekotorye voprosy sovetskoi konstitutsionnoi praktiki"* [Some Problems of Soviet Constitutional Practice], *Sovetskoe gosudarstvo i pravo* [Soviet State and Law], 1956, no. 9, p. 3.

Nikolaichik, V. M., " 'Syvorotka pravdy' i 'lai-detktor'—vozvrashchenie k inkvizitsionnomu protsessu" ['Truth Serum' and the 'Lie Detector'—A Return to the Methods of the Inquisition], *Sovetskoe gosudarstvo i pravo* [Soviet State and Law], 1964, no. 12, p. 120.

Ramundo, Bernard A., "Soviet Criminal Legislation in Implementation of the Hague and Geneva Conventions Relating to The Rules of Land Warfare" *American Journal of International Law,* vol. 57, (1963), p. 63.

Zdir, Ia. A., "O roli gosudarstvennykh inspektsii v obespechenii sotsialisticheskoi zakonnosti v gosudarstvennom upravlenii" [The Role of State Inspection Agencies in the Guaranteeing of Socialist Legality in State Administration], *Sovetskoe gosudarstvo i pravo* [Soviet State and Law], 1964, no. 11, p. 56.

PART II: SUGGESTED SOURCES FOR FURTHER READING

1. *Bibliographies*

A. Soviet

Ratner, L. I., "O sostoianii i dal'neishikh zadachakh bibliographii pravovoi literatury v SSSR" [On the Condition and Further Tasks of Bibliography of Legal Literature in the USSR], *Sovetskoe gosudarstvo i pravo* [Soviet State and Law], 1963, no. 11, pp. 74-84. A comprehensive survey of Russian-language bibliographic materials on Soviet Law.

USSR Academy of Sciences, Institute of State and Law, *Literature on Soviet Law* (Moscow 1960). A selective bibliography of Soviet legal materials published with the aid of UNESCO. Text is in both English and Russian.

B. Non-Soviet

Harvard Law School Library, *Soviet Legal Bibliography, A classified and annotated listing of books and serials published in the Soviet Union since 1917 as represented in the collection of the Harvard Law School Library as of Jan. 1, 1965.* (Vaclav Mostecky and William E. Butler, editors, Cambridge, Mass., 1965).

Hazard, John N., and Isaac Shapiro, *The Soviet Legal System, Post-Stalin Documentation and Historical Commentary* (Dobbs Ferry, N. Y., 1962). Contains excellent bibliographies of books and articles in English on Soviet law.

Meissner, Boris, ed., *Sowjetunion und Volkerrecht,* 1917-1962 (Koln, 1963). An updated German version (with Russian text on facing pages) of a standard Soviet bibliography, with an extensive commentary by the editor.

Osteuropa-Recht (Stuttgart). This journal regularly contains bibliographies of works on Soviet law published outside the USSR.

Ushakow, Alexander, ed., *Das Sowjetische Internationale Privatrecht 1917 bis 1962* (Koln, 1964). An updated German version (with Russian text on facing pages) of a standard Soviet bibliography, with an extensive commentary by the editor.

2. *Works in English on Soviet International Law*

A. Books and Monographs

Akademiia nauk SSSR [Academy of Sciences of the USSR], Institut gosudarstva i prava [Institute of State and Law], *International Law: A Textbook for Use in Law Schools* translated by Dennis Ogden, Moscow, n.d.). An English translation of a 1957 Soviet textbook.

Grzybowski, Kazimierz, *Soviet Private International Law* (Leyden, 1960).

McWhinney, Edward, *"Peaceful Coexistence" and Soviet-Western International Law* (Leyden, 1964).

Ramundo, Bernard A., *The (Soviet) Socialist Theory of International Law* (Washington, D.C., 1964).

Slusser, Robert M. and Jan F. Triska, *A Calendar of Soviet Treaties* 1917-1957 (Stanford, 1959). A comprehensive list of agreements concluded by the Soviet government. Supplements appear in the German journal *Osteuropa-Recht.*

Taracouzio, Timothy A. *The Soviet Union and International Law* (New York, 1945).

Triska, Jan F. and Robert M. Slusser, *The Theory, Law and Policy of Soviet Treaties* (Stanford, 1962).

B. Articles

Ginsburgs, George, "The Validity of Treaties in the Municipal Law of the 'Socialist States,'" *American Journal of International Law,* vol. 59 (1965), p. 523.

Hazard, John N., "The Soviet Union and International Law," *Soviet Studies,* vol. 1 (1950), p. 189.

Korovin, E. A., "International Law Today," *International Affairs* (Moscow), 1961, no. 7, p. 18; "Sovereignty and Peace," *International Affairs* (Moscow), 1960, no. 9, p. 7.

Lay, S. Houston, "The United States—Soviet Consular Convention," *American Journal of International Law,* vol. 59 (1965), p. 876.

Lissitzyn, Oliver J., "The Soviet Union and International Law," in *International Law Today and Tomorrow* (Dobbs Ferry, N.Y., 1965), p. 45.

Maggs, Peter B., "The Soviet Viewpoint on Nuclear Weapons in International Law," *Law and Contemporary Problems,* vol. 29 (1964), p. 956.

Tammelo, Ilmar, "Coexistence and Communication: Theory and Reality in Soviet Approaches to International Law," *Sydney Law Review,* vol. 5 (1965), p. 29.

Tunkin, G. I., "Co-existence and International Law," *Recueil des cours,* vol. 95 (1958), p. 1; "Remarks on the Juridical Nature of Customary Norms of International Law," *California Law Review,* vol. 49 (1961), p. 419; "Some Developments in International Law Concerning Diplomatic Privileges and Immunities," *International Affairs* (Moscow), 1957, no. 12, p. 64.

Zile, Zigurds L., "A Soviet Contribution to International Adjudication: Professor Krylov's Jurisprudential Legacy," *American Journal of International Law,* vol. 58 (1964), p. 359.

TABLE OF ABBREVIATIONS

CDSP—*Current Digest of the Soviet Press*

n.—footnote

TIAS—Treaties and Other International Acts Series

UNTS—United Nations Treaty Series

UST & OIA—United States Treaties and Other International Agreements

Vedomosti—Vedomosti Verkhovnogo Soveta SSSR [*Gazette of the Supreme Soviet of the USSR*]

INDEX

152

153